ATTICS AND BASEMENTS

Make It Right®

ATTICS AND BASEMENTS

MIKE HOLMES

Collins

Make It Right [®]
Attics and Basements
Text copyright © 2011 Restovate Ltd. All rights reserved.

Published by Collins, an imprint of HarperCollins Publishers Ltd

First Canadian edition

HarperCollins books may be purchased for educational, business, or sales promotional use through our Special Markets Department.

HarperCollins Publishers Ltd
2 Bloor Street East, 20th Floor
Toronto, Ontario, Canada
M4W 1A8

www.harpercollins.ca

Library and Archives Canada Cataloguing in Publication

Holmes, Mike
Make it right : attics and basements / Mike Holmes.

ISBN 978-1-55468-031-3

1. Attics—Remodeling. 2. Basements—Remodeling.
I. Title. II. Title: Attics and basements.
TH4816.3.A77H65 2009   643'.5   C2009-903153-1

Printed and bound in Canada
TC 9 8 7 6 5 4 3 2 1

Photography Credits:
Alamy, pp. 24, 26, 32; BASF, p. 56; Mark Bernardi, p. xii; Corbis, pp. 31, 89, 130; Dreamstime, p. 109; FirstLight, pp. 98–99; The Holmes Group, pp. 4–5, 10, 17 (bottom), 18, 38, 73, 77, 81, 83, 102, 104, 113, 122, 132, 135,142; Imagineering Media, p. 17; iStockphoto, pp. 2, 8, 12, 22, 23, 29, 41, 50–51, 65, 70–71, 86, 100, 124; Joseph Marranca, pp. 14, 43, 45, 47, 55, 60, 63, 94, 118; Monika Schurmann, pp. 6, 36.

To the next generation of skilled trades workers—
you will continue to make it right.

CONTENTS

ATTICS AND BASEMENTS

INTRODUCTION

Most of the time people don't call me until all hell breaks loose. One homeowner I met had a contractor who wasn't finishing the job and was threatening to put a lien on the house. Worse, the work was a disaster. The homeowner wanted to put a room in the attic. The contractor told him that he could build a liveable area because the house had a peaked roof, but you can't build that without major structural changes. New homes have prefabricated roofing trusses that are designed to support your roof and the ceiling below. The contractor cut all the roof trusses and started to rebuild the structure in his own way. The damage to the existing structure was phenomenal, and it cost a fortune to turn it into an attic and a liveable zone.

Finishing a basement or attic *the right way* is a major undertaking. As far as I'm concerned, there is no other way to do it. Look at all the "eye candy"—the photos that look great and make renovations seem easy—but don't get stuck there. Just start with it. You've got to educate yourself about your house—what it's got already, what it doesn't, what's possible, what it's going to cost. You've got to find the best contractor your money can buy, which means checking out the candidates by asking a million questions and making sure you know who and what you're getting. Get ideas and get inspired. You can have the bar, the rec room, the extra bedroom—anything you want. But if you want to get the real goods on renos, you've got to go deeper—you've got to look at the world behind the walls. I'm talking about structure, waterproofing, insulation, mechanicals. That's the key to a successful renovation.

This book is going to show you why.

CHAPTER 1

Getting Started

Years ago, when houses were built the basement was never finished as a liveable space like a rec room or even a nanny suite. The whole idea was that the basement held the mechanicals of the house and provided some storage space. The basement was not designed to be watertight or meant to be finished, which meant there would always be easy access for repairs if there were problems with the systems of the house such as plumbing, drains, or electrical.

It wasn't much different with attics. Years ago, attics were just attics, not living spaces. They were just a cold zone and not heated like the rest of the house. The insulation was not the same as it is today, the structure was not the same. The attic was just meant as a place to put in some boxes of stuff after the kids had grown up and moved out.

Now, years later, people want to expand their homes, and they'll take an old house and finish the basement without thinking about the original design. As you plan your renovation, remember the original purpose of these rooms.

Remember too, to slow down. Sometimes people get the idea that a reno can be done in just a few weeks or maybe a month. Well, the good news is that a lot of renos do take that amount of time, or even less. But that's just the time on the site, at your house. That doesn't count all the time it takes to plan everything, find the right contractor, and get the permits you need. In fact, it can take as long, or longer, to find the right contractor than to complete your renovation.

It's important to be realistic about what's ahead of you, so before you pick up the phone and call the first contractor you find online, slow down and educate yourself. Think through every part of the project.

What you see.
What I see.

To you, it may look like there is a lot of wasted space in this basement that could be turned into more living area. I see the mechanicals of the house set up to allow easy access for maintenance and repairs.

This may look like the plumbing system for a house with tankless water heaters and plumbing manifold (which I recommend). It's actually the system for radiant floor heating (which I also recommend). The white boxes are high-efficiency boilers. Hot water is supplied through the plumbing manifold below it.

Two furnaces? They're not furnaces, but HRVs (heating recovery ventilators). The HRVs push fresh air through the house (one HRV is zoned for each floor). Radiant heating should have these systems too. An air cleaner, attached to the HRV, scrubs the air in the house and is a smart choice.

You see a hole in your floor, but I see protection against flooding. A sump pit and sump pump are key parts of the waterproofing system that keeps your basement dry. Let's hope that it drains farther from your house than minimum code requires.

Think about the long term

There are lots of reasons you might decide you need to increase the living space in your home.

For example, if you're going to work from home, you probably need a separate home office. You need a quiet space away from the rest of the family, and maybe a separate entrance so that clients can get to your office without going through your living space.

Maybe you're expecting a new member of the household—a new baby or an older relative. In cases like that, you'll have to consider what that person will need.

If an older relative is joining your household, you might be looking for more than a bedroom. Maybe you want to set up a granny suite to give that person some independence and freedom. That might mean a kitchen and bathroom as well as a living room and bedroom. And, of course, whenever you design a space for an older person, you should consider access: one-level living is best, and the fewer stairs, the better. In fact, the attic or basement means this option is not in the cards—even more reason to plan with care.

Maybe your reno plans have more to do with adding luxury to your home. A home gym, a wine cellar, more recreational space to gather with friends and family? Consider exactly what you want and how much room you'll need.

If what you're looking for is a rental suite in your basement or attic, you've got to meet a lot of building code regulations and other legal requirements. Just as anywhere else in your home, any bedroom, bathroom, or kitchen that you add in a basement or attic must meet all minimum code requirements for plumbing, electrical, HVAC, etc. Electrical outlets in bedrooms must have arc fault breakers for added fire protection. Depending on where you live and the zoning, you may need a separate entrance, and a fire escape in every bedroom, which means a door or a window big enough for someone to climb through. Check with local building authorities and keep in mind that some municipal bylaws prevent residential homes from being converted into apartments.

If you're serious about renting out a unit in your basement or attic, make it legal and make it right. Find out about all your legal obligations from the building department in your municipality—they should have information on which building codes and fire codes apply to you. And check with your mortgage holder and insurance company, too, to be sure that your agreements with them allow you to rent out a suite in your home.

How much is it going to cost?

Budgeting for a reno is also about how much you can afford to spend. How much do you have saved, or how much can you borrow? If you're planning to borrow, visit your bank and find out how much of a renovation loan you could be approved for—before you hire a contractor. Whatever you do, make sure you've got your financing lined up so you'll never have trouble paying your contractor when the time comes.

Always put your own needs first during a renovation, rather than focusing on how much of your investment you'll recoup when you sell your home. Also, pay attention to the houses in your neighbourhood, so you don't make the mistake of overimproving.

Maybe you have no idea how much the job is going to cost. A smart move is to get a ballpark figure from a contractor. This isn't the same thing as asking a contractor to bid on the job. It means bringing in a contractor, maybe for a set fee, to give you a quick assessment of your house and your plans, and let you know a general figure that you should budget for.

At this point, you don't have to have your plans drawn out or your list of materials in hand, but you need to be able to say something like, "We want to turn our attic into a master bedroom suite, with four new windows, a shed dormer, and an ensuite bathroom with a separate shower and bath." That's enough detail for the contractor to give you that ballpark figure.

What can you expect to hear about the cost of finishing a basement or attic?

If you look at it by comparison to building an addition, basements and attics can be a bargain because the basic structure is already there. Where you might pay between $90 and $360 per square foot for the extra space of an addition, you can get the same space in your basement or attic for between $30 and $80 per square foot.

But keep a few things in mind.

First, at $30 per square foot, you're looking at basic-level finishes—carpet or vinyl rather than hardwood, no luxury features in the bathroom, and no built-ins such as bookcases or a home theatre. Obviously, the more you want, the higher the price.

Second, if you do some quick math you'll see that we're talking about big numbers to finish raw space like a basement or attic, even if you don't splurge. At $30 per

Renovating an attic can seem like an inexpensive way to get more space in your house. But keep in mind that, because of limited headroom, you will not gain much liveable space.

square foot, an average basement of 1,000 square feet, including a bathroom, is still going to cost you about $30,000.

Third, if your reno plans will need substantial structural work, such as lowering and underpinning the basement floor, for example, you're looking at much higher costs—probably another $30,000.

So, before you can really figure out how much your plans are going to cost, you need to get some basic info about your house.

That ties into my next point: the structure of your house will tell you a lot about what you need to do, and how much it will cost.

Will the structure of your house add to the cost?

I've seen it happen lots of times. A homeowner hires a contractor to finish their basement, and then there are problems—maybe there's moisture, maybe there are bulkheads running everywhere on the ceiling and you have to duck your head to walk around. When I'm brought in, I find out that the contractor didn't deal with waterproofing issues at all, and tried to get away with a ceiling height that was just too low for a finished basement. Maybe the homeowner wanted the contractor to cut corners, or maybe they didn't know any better. Either way, the homeowner has spent thousands on a basement they can't even use.

There are lots of structural issues that can make it hard to convert a basement or attic into living space. Pretty much anything is possible if you've got the money to

Should you do it yourself?

When you look at the cost of your renovation, you may be thinking about slapping up some studs and drywall yourself to save some money. Basement and attic renos are major projects. They take a lot of specialized skills and experience, as well as good subcontractors like electricians and plumbers to do their part too. What about saving money? Sure, you might save on labour costs, but those savings could be eaten up by expensive tools, extra building materials, and mistakes. Don't underestimate how much work there is still left for you to do in planning your reno. Hire right, let the pros do their jobs, and you won't be disappointed.

spend, but do you have that kind of money, and is that how you want to spend it?

Let's talk about issues in basements first, because it's important to realize that the basement is different than any other area in your house because it's partially below ground. That changes everything.

If your house is an older one, it's possible that the basement has some pretty severe moisture problems, and it might not have the headroom you need to finish it. Does that mean you can't have a finished basement in an older house? No, far from it. But the cost will be higher because to get that extra height you'll probably have to lower the foundation and underpin it, as well as waterproof it. Underpinning involves digging below the existing foundation level, then adding footings at that lower level so the structure of the house is supported. It's a job for professionals only, it's time-consuming, and it's expensive. It can range from $5,000 to $100,000, depending on the size of the building, the depth you want, and access issues, like other houses that are built very close by.

In addition to getting the necessary height, you'll need to be sure that the basement is dry. That will likely mean waterproofing the foundation from the outside. That will also add substantially to the cost (starting at a minimum $10,000 to excavate, waterproof, put in weeping tile, and backfill), but it may be necessary if you want a dry basement for any of the big plans you have in mind.

A basement that's already full height is a better candidate for expansion. Most newer homes will have that full height because the developers expect that many homeowners will finish their basements over time. The foundations of newer houses also have some degree of waterproofing on the exterior—but it may be minimum code, which isn't enough.

Aside from waterproofing and height issues, basements often have very small windows, and may also have fewer doors to the outside than you would like. Larger

Moisture is an important consideration when you're renovating your basement. Using the right product, like BluWood, for structure is a smart way to help prevent mould.

windows are a good idea because you should always have at least one window that's big enough to use as a fire escape, even if it's not required by law. And if you're planning a rental unit in the basement, fire exit windows are necessary by law.

It's possible to change both windows and doors in your basement, but it's not cheap. Foundations are generally made of some form of masonry (poured concrete,

concrete block, or stone), and once again it's specialized and expensive work if you want to have these walls modified. There's also the cost of the interior support that's needed, the window itself, and the drainage and waterproofing around the window well. You should count on an enlarged basement window costing significantly more than a window anywhere else in the house.

In general, keep these points in mind. A basement is a good candidate for renovation if:

- **It has enough headroom to allow a finished floor-to-ceiling height of at least 90 inches. In your calculations, allow at least 2½ inches for flooring and ceiling materials.**
- **It has good waterproofing on the exterior (around the foundation), and there aren't any moisture issues inside.**
- **It has at least one window that's large enough for a fire escape, and a door to the exterior.**

Anything is possible in a renovation, so even if your basement isn't an ideal candidate, you can probably make your plans work. But again it's an issue of money.

Let's say you're more interested in finishing the attic. You'll need to find out how it's constructed.

If your house was built using prefabricated roof trusses, you shouldn't even consider an attic project. The framing members (they look like a bunch of triangles) are there for a reason: they're holding up the roof of your house, and giving the whole structure its stability.

It's technically possible, even with prefabricated trusses, to restructure the roof in a way that gives you open, liveable attic space, but it's in the same category as some other major jobs I've already mentioned: specialized, time-consuming, and expensive. You'll need professional advice from a structural engineer and maybe an architect. You'll need every kind of permit going.

An attic is a good candidate for converted living space if:

- **The roof is supported with standard rafters, not trusses.**
- **There's already stairway access to the attic, or an area on the floor below the attic could be sacrificed to make way for a staircase.**
- **The floor of the attic is already a load-bearing floor.**
- **There's adequate floor space and height available. Most building codes require that at least half the floor area of any room used as living space have a minimum ceiling height of 90 inches. Adding dormers is a common way to increase the amount of floor space with that minimum height.**

Prefabricated and carefully engineered roofing trusses are used in new home construction. These trusses are designed to support the ceiling below the roof, not a floor. You can't mess with these supports unless you are working with a structural engineer.

There are some forms of trusses that are "attic-type" roof trusses. They use the principles of truss design, but are modified to leave enough space open for finished rooms.

Building code requirements

Building codes are pretty standard across North America, but every municipality will have its own version. Legally, the responsibility for meeting code requirements falls on your shoulders as the homeowner, rather than the contractor's. If an engineer, architect, or registered interior designer is working with you, they'll be familiar with the codes and will make sure that all requirements are met. If you're working without professional help like this, get to know the people at your municipality's building and planning department. They can advise you on the rules and regulations that will affect your project.

Building permits are always needed when the work involves structural changes. They're needed for additions of any kind, for electrical work, for plumbing work (though not if you're just replacing existing plumbing fixtures such as a sink or toilet), and often for finishing basements and attics. Basement lowering, adding and removing windows or doors, and adding a fireplace are other examples of when you'll need a permit—and, more importantly, when your plans need to satisfy the requirements of the building code.

Getting permits isn't that difficult or expensive, and ultimately those permits are there to protect you. Never look at a permit as an inconvenience. It's there as a form of insurance for you. If your contractor tries to get away with shoddy work, or if they just don't know what they're doing, the municipal inspector who follows through on the permit should spot the problems.

Once you have a permit, a municipal inspector will come to your home a number of times throughout your renovation (the exact number depends on the work being done). I strongly advise you to be at these inspections, and to ask the inspector questions.

Always get permits for the work being done in your home. Don't take a contractor's word that a permit isn't needed: check it out with the municipality yourself. Just let them know what you plan to have done, and they'll tell you if a permit is needed or not. If you do need a permit, don't even think about working with any contractor who said you didn't. Getting a permit is the cheapest and best form of insurance you'll ever buy.

No matter what you have in mind, just remember there are lots of building code regulations and bylaws that could affect your decisions. And as I mentioned earlier, this is definitely true if you want to put an entire rental suite into your home. Don't mess around with the regulations around rentals. You could find yourself slapped with a very hefty fine, and you could run into big problems with your insurance company. And if you don't follow the fire code regulations, you could end up with a fire that causes major damage—or even death—because you couldn't be bothered to check into the rules.

Wherever you decide to spend your reno dollars, make sure you do the project right. Unfortunately, I've seen again and again that it's very possible to spend thousands of dollars and still end up with a reno that's total crap.

It really doesn't have to be that way. A renovation should be a great opportunity to make your house into a place you love—if you get it done right. In the following chapters of this book, I'm going to guide you through the main components of any basement or attic conversion project, and you'll see what I mean.

CHAPTER 2

Structure, Waterproofing, and Insulation

The next stage in the process is determining the scope of the job. The scope refers to the extent of the project. How much will be done, how far under the surface will you go, how will the space be finished, and how much is it all going to cost?

It's time to take an inventory of the major components and systems in your house. You have to assess what you currently have, and then figure out where you want to get to. In this chapter, we'll cover the topics of structure, waterproofing, and insulation. In the next chapter, we'll look at the mechanicals of the house: electrical, plumbing, and HVAC. For some of these items, you don't need any help to figure out what you've got—you just need to spend the time looking, doing some research, and writing down some facts and figures. For other items, you need expert guidance, such as a structural engineer, a plumber, an electrician, and/or a very experienced general contractor.

A reliable home inspector can also be a great place to start. Home inspectors are generalists rather than specialists, and for a relatively small fee you can get a pretty good idea of the type of systems you've got in your home and what kind of shape they're in. But do your homework—get lots of references and check them out—before hiring to make sure you're getting someone with lots of experience as a home inspector, and preferably someone who was in the building trades before that.

Structure

The first rule of any home renovation project—from the basement to the attic and everywhere in between—should be this: don't compromise structure. Just like the bones in our body, the frame in a house holds everything up. A frame that's starting to sag means trouble. Every well-built house—whether old or new—starts out right: on a solid foundation, with structural and bearing walls level and true, and with point loads accurately calculated. A house frame is full of joints and fasteners, and any weak points can act like a hinge. Weak points can happen because of age or previous "home improvements" where someone cuts out joists—or even beams—and compromises the structure in a renovation. They make "educated" guesses about structural members, or about what the current bearing load on a wall is, or that some other wall can take a lot more load than it has.

And for a time you might not even notice, but believe me, the house is affected. The house might even have a second renovation—with more of the same types of changes to the structure. And what you end up with is cracks in the plaster, buckling drywall, windows and doors that stick—houses that lean, houses with floors that sag and slope, or, even worse, houses that fall down.

Probably the most dangerous place of all to make structural changes is in the basement, because anything you do there will be felt through every level of the house. How do you know if it's safe or advisable to make an adjustment to the structure? The truth is—you don't. A good contractor does. An architect does. A structural engineer does. If any structural changes are required for the project you want to undertake—and they probably will be—you should consult one or more of these pros before finalizing your plans.

Remember that all structural issues are important because they involve the safety of your home and the safety of your family. Structural issues are governed by building codes. If you try to go around the code, or work without a permit, you'll be in violation of the code and the regulations in your region, and you could find yourself with a hefty fine or a stop-work order. That will mean calling a halt to your project until the problems are solved—if they can be. In other words, if structural issues can't be dealt with, the deal is off.

Structural issues in the basement

There are three main issues that determine whether or not your basement is a good candidate for conversion: headroom, waterproofing, and access.

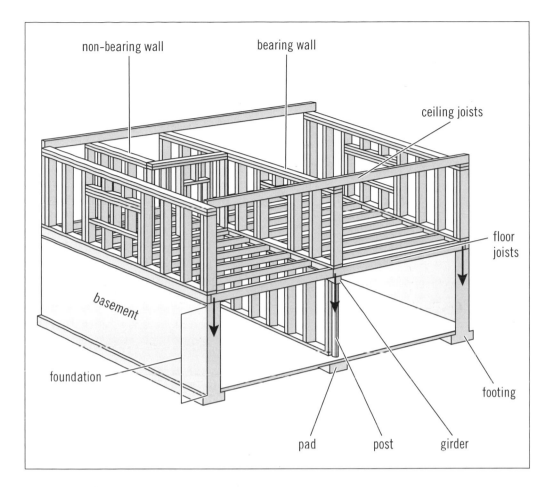

non-bearing wall

bearing wall

ceiling joists

floor joists

basement

foundation

footing

pad

post

girder

The only way to know for sure if a wall is bearing or non-bearing is to hire a structural engineer. The general rule of thumb, though, is that all loads need to be carried continuously down to the footings (top). Whatever you do, don't mess with structure or you could end up with a costly repair (bottom).

Headroom

A basement shouldn't feel cramped, with ceilings that make you feel claustrophobic. If you spend all kinds of money and still end up with a basement that has low ceilings where you feel like you might bump your head, I guarantee you'll be sorry.

How much height is enough? Most building codes require the height to be at least 90 inches (7 feet 6 inches) to be considered living space. In your calculations, allow at least 2½ inches for flooring and ceiling materials.

If you don't have that minimum height, you can have the basement floor lowered. Lowering a basement floor is a huge job. It needs to be professionally done by an experienced and skilled foundation expert or contractor. You will absolutely need a building permit, and professional drawings (drawn and stamped by a licensed structural engineer) to get the permit. If any contractor says you won't need a permit to do this kind of work, you can end the conversation right there, because they don't know what they're talking about.

Lowering a floor can be done in two ways: underpinning or bench-pinning. Either way, it's an expensive job. The quotes you get will depend on a number of factors: the size (square footage) of the area to be worked on, how deep you want to go, landscaping and soil issues around the foundation, site access, and the weather you might encounter.

Some of those factors are obviously going to affect the cost, such as square footage and depth. The less obvious factors are things like soil, which will need to be removed and dumped. Your contractor might be able to use a conveyor to carry the

Lowering a basement is labour intensive and needs to be done slowly and carefully.

soil out of your basement, or it may have to be carried by hand in buckets. And if the soil is heavy clay, or even rock, you've got a more difficult job on your hands.

If you live in an older or inner-city area, your house may be very close to your neighbours' houses. The contractor will have to ensure that the work being done doesn't affect the stability of your neighbours' foundations. And you'll need to talk to your neighbours on either side to reassure them the work will be done safely and legally, and won't compromise the structural integrity of their homes.

Let's talk a bit more about underpinning. It's done by working in small sections (about 3 feet at a time) around the perimeter of the basement wall. The contractor excavates the soil around the foundation wall, removes the original footings, and then pours new footings at a lower depth than the original footings. The wall itself is then rebuilt in sections. The load has to be carefully transferred and supported because what you're doing is temporarily undermining the house's foundation—in a controlled way—in order to rebuild it.

The finished interior basement wall will be flush top to bottom. After the deeper walls are finished, the basement floor will be dug out to the new depth to provide the ceiling height you're after.

What about benchpinning? It costs less than underpinning because it doesn't require digging under the existing footings—the existing footings and soil remain untouched. There's less soil removal, and the job is quicker. The soil stays in place under the original footings, and a new foundation is poured inside the existing one—on the inside of your basement walls—down to the new depth.

Bench-pinning does make the basement smaller, since the perimeter walls now will have a concrete "bench" all along them. For every foot you go down in depth, you must add a foot in width to the bench. So if you're dropping the floor 2 feet, you'll have a 2' wide bench along the base of your new wall—which of course will affect how you can use that basement room.

Whether you need underpinning or bench-pinning, the contractor you choose is the most important choice you'll make. The right contractor is always important, but never more so than when you're making changes to your foundation. Do not take any chances when working on your foundation! Do your homework and find the right contractor—someone with a lot of experience on foundations. Stay away from anyone who can start tomorrow. And check references—lots and lots of them. Ask to see the work that was done, and ask homeowners if they've noticed any problems since the work was done.

Waterproofing

Moisture—and its best friend, mould—is the biggest enemy in the basement. It's a waste of your time and money to finish a basement unless all moisture issues have been dealt with.

The best way to control moisture is from the outside. If your foundation doesn't already have adequate waterproofing (which is likely to be the case with older houses), the price tag for your basement reno is going to get bigger—a lot bigger.

Exterior waterproofing jobs are the ideal way to prepare for a finished basement, but they'll cost quite a few thousand dollars, depending on the size of your house and the difficulty of accessing those exterior walls.

Access

Everybody loves big windows, and adding or enlarging windows is part of a lot of renovation plans these days. In a basement, a legal rental unit requires a window that's big enough for a person to escape in case of fire, and even if you're not planning to rent out your basement you should have a window like this. It's all about safety. (Check with your local building authorities to find out what size is required.)

But enlarging or adding a window to a basement is much more complicated than anywhere else in your house.

Windows and doors in the basement are simply holes in the foundation, and because the foundation is so important to the structure of your house, any changes have to be done right.

Think about the fact that any window or door needs to be supported from above and below. When houses are built, windows and doors are framed in with adequate support—the framing ensures that the load is transferred to the walls on either side of the window or door. The weight of the building structure can't rest on a window or door frame.

This is even more important if you're enlarging a window or door in a foundation wall. Most foundations are made of masonry—poured concrete, concrete block, or stone. You can't just remove a section of a masonry wall and expect the structure to stay intact.

What about that walk-out from the basement you've been imagining? Just like with that new window, you have the same concern with structure above the doorway, and if exterior stairs are needed up to ground level, they'll need to be built with the same kind of support as the foundation itself, footings and all.

Whenever you go below grade (also called ground level)—with that walkout or a larger window, for example—you're going to have drainage challenges. Your contractor has to be experienced and knowledgeable enough to drain the areas under the window and door with a vertical run of tile that's connected to the existing weeping tile at the footings of your foundation.

I once had to rescue a newly "finished" basement where everything had been done wrong. One of the worst things was the way the contractor had enlarged the basement windows. He had no idea what he was doing, and he had no business being there in the first place. He'd installed the windows without any lintels above them, and the window wells were so sloppy that I guarantee you they would have brought water into that basement during the first good storm.

We had to take everything apart inside the basement, and start from scratch on the window wells.

Here's what has to be done whenever you enlarge a basement window that will be set above the level of the existing window and will also extend below grade:

- **Bricks above the window have to be removed so that a proper lintel can be installed. The lintel is the horizontal support that spans the top of the window, and it has to extend at least 6 inches on either side of the window to carry the structural load. Lintels can also be made from concrete (poured in place or precast), stone, or steel. For retrofits, an angle iron lintel probably makes the most sense—it's easiest to install, and the cost is reasonable.**
- **The floor joists (inside the house) have to be restructured to help carry the load.**
- **Before installing the window well, a trench has to be dug in front of the window right down to the weeping tile. This is found at the lowest point of the foundation. A hole is cut into the top of the weeping tile and a vertical section of tile is attached. This vertical section will drain the water from the base of the window well.**
- **While the trench is open, the foundation wall can be waterproofed with several layers of waterproofing: a trowel coat of mastic, a layer of fabric mesh, another coat of mastic, a sheet of 3-mil plastic pushed tight against the mastic, and finally an outer layer of dimpled plastic membrane. The dimpled plastic has to be properly tied into existing membrane to ensure waterproofing is continuous.**
- **The window well can now be installed, and the whole area can be backfilled with gravel that contains as little soil as possible. The top edge of the dimpled plastic wrap should not be covered.**

You can probably see by now that even a "small" job like enlarging a window is actually a pretty big one. The total cost of a job like this could be much more than you expected—as much as several thousand dollars once you include the excavation, waterproofing, drainage, masonry, the window well, and of course, the window itself.

What else do you need to know about structure in the basement?

The wide-open spaces of basements are often a big reason that people love to turn them into living space. But just remember that most existing supports—such as walls, columns, or floor-to-ceiling posts of any kind—are there for a reason. Don't remove them just to get that spacious feeling. That's a sure-fire way to undermine the structure of your house.

Instead, consult a structural engineer to determine what kind of support you really need in the basement. They can tell you which walls are supporting (other than the obvious exterior walls), and which are unnecessary. They can point out any areas where

If posts or other structural supports are necessary in your basement renovation, you can make them part of your design.

the joists might have been compromised in the past (especially by cutting into the lower parts of the joist to run plumbing or wiring), and how these areas should be fixed.

They can also tell you where support posts need to be kept, or added. And never let a contractor tell you that a support post can be put up directly on your basement floor without addressing the question of footings. Any support post needs to have a concrete footing under it. The building code requires it—not to mention common sense. How can a post support your house if it's not standing on something solid?

Structural issues in the attic

Next to the basement, the attic is the most likely area for home expansion. It's already part of the building structure, and it should have fewer moisture problems than you'll encounter in a basement. If the basic structure is solid and suitable for a finished attic, you could have the solution to your space problem just overhead.

Attics offer more than square footage. When you build into the roof area, you're bound to get some really interesting ceiling angles and lines that will add aesthetic value to the space. You can have the cathedral ceiling that so many people want. And the higher you move up in the house, the more privacy, unobstructed views, and sunlight you get.

For all the positive things about attics, though, there can be drawbacks, at least as far as structure is concerned. Most attics require at least some structural work to make them into living space. Others need a lot. And in some cases, it just shouldn't be attempted at all. Let's look first at the worst-case scenario so we can get that over with.

Here's a classic example of when it just doesn't make sense to try to build into your attic. Earlier in this book, I recommended that you not even consider an attic project if

You don't want to take shortcuts with structure in an attic. Any changes have to be done carefully and should be approved by a structural engineer.

your house was built using prefabricated roof trusses, which is usually the case with newly built homes or many houses built after the war, especially since the 1970s.

That can be disappointing, because even from the outside you can see that there's lots of room up there, right? Wrong.

Trusses cannot be removed without endangering the structure of the entire house. They're built using 2×4s, usually placed 24 inches on centre, with diagonal bracing that takes the place of the support provided by traditional rafters. Those trusses are there to do only two things: hold up the roof and keep the walls of your house from moving out. They're not meant to support a floor or furniture or people. And without those trusses—even just a few of them—there's not enough support for your roof or your walls.

If your house is built with trusses, don't even think about an attic room. Consider an addition to another part of your house. It will cost you a lot less money, time, and headaches. And you won't have to worry that your house will fall in because someone messed up the whole structure that supports it.

In the previous chapter, I listed the various points that would make an attic a good candidate for conversion to living space. I want to look at each of those points

A large dormer can add light, height, and more livable space to your attic.

again, with more detail so you can understand the importance of each one, and see for yourself if your attic has what it takes.

Rafters, not trusses

If you have rafters, from the inside of your attic you'll be able to see wooden framing members directly under the roof, following the roof line. There may be some uprights as well, either close to the outer edges of the roof, or directly under the peak of the roof. Another possibility is that you'll see "collar ties," which are horizontal members that connect the rafters for stability (usually fairly close to the top of the roof, which is called the ridge). All of these are critical to the structure. If they're removed, they'll have to be compensated for with some other form of support.

Stairway access

It's best if there's already stairway access to the attic, or you can easily identify an area below the attic that could be sacrificed to make way for a staircase. A pull-down staircase can't legally be used to access a finished attic.

If you have to build a staircase, be aware that even though building codes vary (and you should check with your municipality's building department to be sure), all codes will require similar minimum dimensions for stairs. The requirements are all about safety. Here's a list of the basics:

- **The stairway must be at least 36 inches wide between finished walls.**
- **If the stairs have nosings (the rounded, overhanging section on each stair tread), they cannot project more than 1½ inches.**
- **The minimum allowable height is 6 feet 8 inches from the top of each step to the finished ceiling (or any other obstruction) above it.**
- **Risers can't be more than 8¼ inches high. The ideal height is 7 inches.**
- **Treads can't be less than 9 inches deep.**
- **If the stairs have three or more risers, you'll need a handrail on at least one side of the staircase.**
- **Landings have to be the same width as the stairs and at least as long as they are wide.**

If you have to add or rebuild the attic stairs to meet code requirements, keep in mind that this will add substantially to your costs. It could mean losing space—and having to pay for additional modifications—on the floor below. It also takes careful planning, and the advice of a structural engineer, to ensure that any staircase you add is framed properly so that it doesn't compromise the overall structure of the house.

Load-bearing floor

In some older homes, you can see the exposed framing members on the "floor" of the attic—these are really just ceiling joists for the rooms below. In some older homes, attics were used as storage space, so you may see floorboards of some kind covering the joists. But just because you see floorboards you shouldn't assume that the floor is "load-bearing."

What does "load-bearing" mean, anyway? There's no simple answer to that because floor and ceiling joists are sized to handle different types of loads. Loads can be divided into "dead" and "live." Dead loads are static—they don't move. The weight of the building itself, including the lumber and finish materials used, is the dead load. Live loads, such as furniture and people, can change. To be used as living space, a floor has to be able to support both dead and live loads.

When older homes were built, the attics were seen either as empty space or light storage space, not as living space. So the joists up there were probably designed to support only the structure of the house (the dead load), which is calculated at 10 pounds per square foot (psf) of floor space. If a room is going to be used as a bedroom, it has to be able to withstand live loads of 30 psf, and other uses require 40 psf.

How can you calculate this? I don't recommend that you try to do this yourself. A structural engineer is the best person to evaluate the load-bearing ability of your attic floor.

They will measure the following:

- **Joist dimensions. The width and depth of the joists is an indication of strength—the bigger, the better.**
- **Joist span. The span is the distance between supports under the joists. Floor joists usually rest on an exterior wall of the house and on an interior wall. (You can see why it's so important not to remove interior walls without expert advice!)**
- **Joist spacing. The closer the joists are set, the stronger the floor will be.**

If your attic floor needs to be beefed up to support living space—and it probably will—the engineer will likely recommend that your contractor do one or more of the following to reinforce it:

- **Add more joists of the same depth as the existing ones.**
- **Add more joists that are deeper than the existing ones.**
- **"Sister" the existing joists by attaching equal-sized joists alongside them.**

If the floor is strong enough, but still moves or bounces when you walk on it, the joists can be stiffened by laminating plywood on either side with both glue and screws.

Floor space and height

Just as with stairs, there are some pretty basic building code rules for floor space and headroom in attics. Check with your local building department to get the specifics in your area, but start with this list:

- **Any attic living space must have a minimum area of 70 square feet, and it must measure no less than 7 feet in every horizontal direction.**
- **At least half the floor space in any room must have a minimum ceiling height of 90 inches (7 feet 6 inches).**
- **Any portions of the room that are less than 5 feet high are not considered living space. These areas at the base of the sloping walls can make good storage space, though.**

You can take a quick measurement to determine if your attic has enough headroom: measure the distance from the ridge (or the underside of the collar ties) to the top of the floor joists. If it doesn't show at least 7 feet 7½ inches (the extra 1½ inches allows for the thickness of a finished ceiling and floor), you can't convert the attic without major work and expense.

If you do want to convert the attic, what are your options for meeting the code requirements? Well, you could raise the roof—but this is a huge and very expensive job. The more common solution is to add dormers, which have a number of advantages: they can make the attic feel more spacious and bring in lots of daylight; they can make the exterior of the house more attractive if they're well designed; and they're relatively easy to add, at least by comparison to some other things you might do.

Dormer designs to expand your attic

Dormers can be the answer to your space dilemma in the attic. Many types of dormers can be useful in gaining more headroom and usable floor space because they raise the roof in parts of the attic. When you add dormers, you have to take into account both practicality and looks. Although there are many different dormer styles, there are really only two basic types: gable dormers and shed dormers. Everything else is just a variation on these two styles. Gable dormers are more common and usually have a window in them, but they don't offer much additional living space. Shed dormers are generally wider, so they give you more headroom and interior space. Regardless of the style you choose, adding a dormer affects the structure of your roof and your house. Plan carefully, get a permit, and make sure your contractor is experienced. You don't want to mess around when it comes to cutting a hole in your roof. How large the dormers are and where they're positioned in your roof will make a difference to how they look.

The dormer(s) you choose should take into account the following:

- **How much usable floor space do you need to gain for your project to get the green light from building authorities?**
- **How much usable floor space do you need to suit the purpose you have in mind (master bedroom, home office, home gym, etc.)?**
- **What type of dormer will suit the style of your house? Do some research about your house's style or consult an architect to help you determine this. You can have the architect do drawings that show several alternatives before making your decision.**
- **The cost of each type of dormer. Gable dormers are more difficult to build, so of course they're more expensive. Shed dormers are not only easier to build, they also give you more usable space, so they give you the most bang for your buck, but they don't have the traditional look of a gable dormer.**

When installing dormers, you need to insulate and waterproof them properly.

Here are just a few suggestions:

- **Align dormer windows with the windows below them, or with the spaces between the windows below.**
- **Make dormers large enough to be worth the trouble and to gain the floor space you need, but not so large that they overwhelm the exterior of the house.**
- **For maximum space in an attic, consider putting dormers on both the front and back of the house. To keep the house from looking top-heavy, put gable dormers on the front and a long shed dormer in back.**
- **Make dormers look natural by using the same roofing as you have on the rest of the house. Use the same type of siding as well, or something that complements the exterior.**

Here's a really important point: if they're not insulated and waterproofed properly, dormers can cause problems with water infiltration, and with condensation and ice dams on the exterior. So what should you do?

The first step is to have closed-cell polyurethane foam insulation applied to the dormer structure before finishing with drywall. You'll create a complete thermal break, which will keep hot and cold from meeting and causing condensation, and you'll also have a built-in vapour barrier. Finally, make sure the roof is finished with the best quality underlayment and with careful attention to the flashing over dormer hips and in valleys.

Other windows and skylights in the attic

Attics that were previously unfinished usually don't have much in the way of windows. You might find a gable vent or a small window that was only intended for ventilation purposes. Dormer windows will bring in a fair bit of light, but what if dormers aren't part of your plan?

You still have options.

Gable (end) walls can be punctured for windows—as long as the structure allows it. Many houses have non-bearing end walls, since the rafters usually carry the whole load of the roof onto the exterior walls. This is the ideal situation if you want windows to bring in natural light.

You'll have more of a challenge if your house is built with a structural ridge beam. What this means is that the ridge beam (which is the main horizontal member at the peak of the roof) supports the top end of each rafter, rather than the other way around. At either end of the ridge beam, in the gable ends, there will a bearing post that supports the beam. You can't put a window dead centre because the beam is in the way,

The wood panel on the ceiling looks good, but is it just strapped to the underside of the roof? If so, that's not good. You need proper insulation and ventilation to protect the structure of your roof.

This stack runs through the middle of the room, which may be unavoidable. But more important, is it in good shape or is it leaking unpleasant odours, or worse, dangerous gasses?

You see an exposed brick chimney. I want to know if it's connected to a furnace or fireplace. If so, is the liner in good shape so no gases leak out? Is there a working carbon monoxide detector in the room?

You see a window seat with a view, but I wonder how this room is being heated and cooled. There is typically a floor register near the window. It's important not to cover up vents or cold air returns.

What you see.
What I see.

and that beam can't be changed without completely redesigning the structure of the house. It is possible, though, to install windows on either side of that bearing post.

How can you tell what kind of structure you've got? You probably can't, but a structural engineer or architect can. This is another reason why getting an assessment from one of these professionals is a good place to start your reno plans. You can find out what you've got to work with, and how complicated—and expensive—it's going to be to install windows in those gable walls.

The other option for natural light is skylights. I think of skylights as "green" features because they allow you to switch off your lights in the daytime and reduce energy use. Skylights actually can provide over three times as much light as a vertical window of the same size, because the light from directly above is stronger than from the horizon.

A skylight is basically a hole in your roof, with a window in it. But if it's not installed professionally you'll have the worst of both window and roof problems—condensation, heat loss in winter, overheating in summer, and leaks. I like to see

Curb-mounted skylights are your best choice in your attic. Placed above the surface of the roof, they're less likely to leak when properly installed.

curb-mounted skylights with Low-E (low emissivity) glass for the best thermal protection. Curb-mounted skylights are probably the ones that are least likely to be badly installed because they're placed above the surface of the roof. Whatever skylight you choose, make sure it's installed 100% correctly by a pro—there's no room for error when you're making a hole in your roof.

Here are some things that are useful to know if you're planning on using skylights in your attic:

- **If you're planning to use the attic as a bedroom, the fire code says you must have a window that can be used as a fire escape. A skylight doesn't fit the bill, so don't think you've met the code requirements by installing one.**
- **Curb-mounted skylights—whether glass or plastic—are a smart choice because they place the skylight higher than the surface of the roof. The skylight is then flashed properly, which seals it and prevents the roof from leaking.**
- **Often people find water damage they think comes from a leaky skylight, and it turns out the cause is condensation build-up. Just like with windows on your walls, your windows in the roof—your skylights—will gather condensation from the air in your home. But instead of pooling on your windowsill, the condensation will drip onto your floors, or run down ceilings and walls. This problem is caused by poor air circulation and high levels of humidity in your house.**
- **In cold climates, frost can form on the inside of your skylight, which will drip when it thaws. Newer, high-quality skylights are better designed and made from new materials using gaskets and thermal breaks to reduce frost build-up.**
- **Skylights can be a source of heat loss as your warm inside air escapes through the roof in winter. And in summer they can create a lot of solar heat gain—which might cost you since you've got to run your air conditioning to compensate. Tinted or light-reflective glass will reduce overheating, but it may also reduce the amount of daylight that comes in. Louvered blinds can be installed to direct the light, but still let it in.**
- **If you get a skylight that can open, use it! Hot air builds up near the ceilings—opening a skylight releases the hot air and allows cooler air to be pushed up from below. Remember that cold air always pushes hot.**
- **A skylight will never be as well insulated as your roof. It can't be. But a well-made skylight can minimize both heat loss in winter and heat gain in summer. Most skylights are now made with Low-E glass for greater thermal efficiency.**

Staircase solutions

Gaining proper access to the attic takes more than just a ladder or a narrow old set of stairs. To get approval to use your attic as living space, and to make the best use of it, you need a real set of stairs. Just imagine trying to get a desk or a queen-size bed up the little flight of stairs that might be in place now.

To get the full-sized stairs you need will take some imagination and ingenuity—and the advice of an architect or engineer. A number of different stair configurations are possible, and if you're lucky you'll be able to make one fit without major changes to the layout on the floor below the attic.

Here are the various possibilities, and some pros and cons for each.

Straight-run stairs are the easiest to build, especially if they run parallel to the ceiling joists above them. To connect one standard-height (8-foot) storey to the next you should expect a straight run of stairs to take up about 40 square feet of floor space. It can be completely enclosed or one side can be open to the room below, with a banister for safety.

L-shaped or U-shaped stairs take up more total floor area, but they may be the solution where a straight run of stairs would be too steep.

Winder stairs are similar to L-shaped stairs, but there's no landing—the transitional steps (the ones that turn the corner) are wedge-shaped. That can be a problem for safety, since the smaller ends of those wedges are too narrow to step on.

Spiral stairs are fun to look at, but not that easy to use. It's also difficult to get large objects up and down them. The main advantage of spiral stairs is how little room they take up—generally about 4 to 6 feet in diameter. But in some areas, the building code won't allow spiral stairs leading up to rooms that are larger than 400 square feet. Check your local code before including spiral stairs in your plans.

Knee walls—for structure or storage?

Another structural question that needs to be addressed is how you'll use the space above the eaves. Remember that any part of the room that is less than 5 feet in height is not considered living space as far as building codes are concerned.

You don't actually have to do anything with these low-ceilinged areas, if you like the look of the triangular shaped attic room or if you think knee walls will make the room feel cramped. But keep in mind that you can get lots of valuable storage space out of them.

Knee walls don't usually have any structural purpose because the rafters above them carry the load of the roof onto the exterior walls of the house. In some cases, though, the roof needs extra support and those knee walls can become part of the structure. If you've already hired an engineer or architect to advise on the floor and staircase, ask about knee walls as well, since any structural wall has to be designed to not only carry the loads but also transfer them to parts of the house that can bear them.

If the knee walls don't need to be structural, you've got a lot of choices about how to use the space behind them. Think about built-in bookshelves, storage cabinets with doors, or filing drawers that roll out on wheels.

Of course, the space behind knee walls has to be insulated if you're going to use it, even for storage. Get closed-cell polyurethane foam sprayed on the underside of the roof (and any uprights), and you'll have created an airtight, well-insulated area that can be finished and used any way you like.

Waterproofing and insulating the basement

Even more than structural issues, moisture issues are a big concern in basements. The problems can range in severity from periodic dampness or excess humidity (in the hot summer months, for instance) to foundation cracks that leak or standing water.

However severe the problem may be, there's just no point in finishing your basement until the moisture problems have been stopped at the source, because that moisture is going to continue to be a problem. Water damage and mould will ruin your investment.

How do you know if there's a problem? Check for the following:

- **foundation cracks that leak**
- **standing water**
- **efflorescence (white, chalky stains) on the walls or floor**
- **wet or decaying wood in contact with concrete**
- **damp or mouldy walls or floor**
- **condensation on windows, pipes, and other fixtures**
- **wet insulation**
- **musty or damp smells**
- **high humidity**

Dealing with water problems at the source

Basements get wet for a lot of reasons.

The first major reason is hydrostatic pressure. Water will always find its way to the lowest point, and it can create a huge amount of pressure on whatever it finds in its path. You have to understand that concrete, which is what most foundations are made of, is actually quite porous. That's why water is able to make its way through the concrete walls and into your basement.

Before starting a basement renovation, walk around your house and look for cracks in the foundation. Small cracks can become bigger and let water leak through.

When hydrostatic pressure builds up enough, small cracks in the foundation will appear, allowing water to seep in even more quickly—and the longer those cracks are neglected, the larger they'll get.

What else can cause water and dampness problems in the basement? Here's a short list:

- **A quick thaw in spring or heavy rains can cause the water table to rise suddenly, overwhelming a home's exterior drainage system. Because the water table is always there, around the house, basement floors are often a really big problem area for moisture.**
- **Incorrectly installed landscaping or poor grading may be directing water to the walls of your home.**
- **Weeping tile—which is designed to collect water and direct it to a sump pump or storm sewer—can get damaged by tree roots or clogged by silt.**
- **Sump pumps fail and if there's no backup in place, you have no way of removing water that's passed through your foundation walls.**
- **If the sump pump drains too close to the foundation wall (it should empty at least a few metres from the house), the water being pumped out of your basement will go right back in.**
- **Your foundation may have little or no exterior water protection, or there may be a problem with the protection that's there.**

MIKE'S TIP

Pay attention to larger cracks.

The cracks we see in basement (foundation) walls are often minor and caused by hydrostatic (water) pressure over time. They must be filled and sealed before finishing your basement, and the source of the water penetration must be found and dealt with so the problem doesn't return. An exterior drainage and waterproofing system is ideal for sealing minor cracks and protecting the foundation from future problems.

But what if the cracks are more substantial?

First of all, never hire a "basement waterproofing specialist" to repair large cracks. It's unlikely they'll be specialists in diagnosing the reason that large cracks have appeared in the first place, or in offering you a real solution to the problem. Waterproofing specialists are great at sealing foundation walls, but major cracks are not their area.

If you see a crack that's ¼" wide or wider, a crack that suddenly increases in size, or cracks in a wall that is bulging, bowing, or leaning, get on the phone to a structural engineer immediately to determine the cause. These are indications of a serious structural problem.

Don't mess with structural issues, and don't ignore them. With any building, there's the possibility of what engineers would call "catastrophic building failure." That means houses can actually fall down.

There are always signs before catastrophes like this take place. Pay attention to the signs, and don't go for the cheap fix.

Whatever the reason, if water or moisture is getting into your basement, you need to take a closer look at your foundation and drainage systems before attempting an interior renovation.

The solution to a water or moisture problem, almost always, is to fix it from the outside. An exterior drainage system is the best drainage system you can get because it's the only one that keeps water from entering your home. Generally, it consists of weeping tile at the base of the foundation and several layers of waterproofing materials applied to the foundation. When installed properly, these give your home a strong defense against water. Let's look at weeping tile first, then move on to the waterproofing part of the equation.

Weeping tile

Weeping tile can be installed only once the soil has been excavated (removed) from the sides of the foundation. This is work for foundation professionals, who will likely use a backhoe to remove the soil, and will brace the foundation properly until the soil can be filled back in. The whole process can be pretty challenging when you consider the number of access issues that could get in the way—everything from a paved driveway alongside the house, to a neighbour's house that's very close to yours, to landscaping that has to be removed, to porches and stairs, etc.

In North America, most weeping tile consists of 4" to 6" plastic perforated piping that's installed around the perimeter of the exterior foundation walls. Its purpose is

Here, the floor drain didn't work properly because it was tied to the weeping tile. The concrete had to be removed so the drain could be connected to the house's main drainage system.

to collect water that drains down the exterior foundation wall and to divert the water into a sump pit or the sewer system before it can be absorbed by the foundation walls. By doing this, weeping tile also helps reduce hydrostatic pressure against the walls and basement floors that could cause your walls to buckle or bow and eventually crack.

Because water will also wash sand and silt towards the weeping tile, the holes can become clogged, making them ineffective. If you find clay weeping tile (from a previous generation), replace it. It's only a matter of time before it cracks or breaks and becomes completely useless. What you want is a weeping tile that's covered in a sock-like fabric—this helps keep silt out of the perforations in the tile. Laying about 3 feet of crushed stone and gravel on top of and around the weeping tile filters even more silt from the water. This method is above code, and I like it because it works.

Weeping tile should be installed so that the top of the piping is level with the interior concrete floor. Once it's in place, the walls of the foundation should be power washed or cleaned with wire brushes to clear them of any debris or dirt. Any minor cracks should be repaired at this point, too, using an injection of hydraulic cement or a non-shrinkable grout. Then it's time for waterproofing.

Waterproofing foundation walls

When it comes to waterproofing, it's important to understand that there are "damp-proof" coatings and "waterproof" coatings. There's a big difference.

A damp-proof coating is usually a black tar or asphalt compound that comes in a bucket and gets painted or rolled onto concrete foundations. This is followed by a mastic paste, a mesh coat, then another coat of mastic. It's a relatively inexpensive system, which explains its popularity, but it will not 100% waterproof your foundation. It's designed to stop water vapour transmission through your concrete foundation walls. It won't stand up to hydrostatic pressure and also won't bridge tiny cracks that might already exist in your foundation walls.

It's far better to use a waterproof coating. I like a two-coat liquid rubberized membrane. It's sprayed on by certified contractors, and creates an instant-set membrane that cures into a rubbery 100% waterproof coating. It will stop all water infiltration into the porous concrete foundation walls by forming a membrane that stretches and allows for settling of the house over time. There's a wide variety of waterproofing products like this on the market, and they're more expensive than damp-proofing, but they're worth it because they have some resistance to hydrostatic pressure.

Whether you use damp-proofing materials or a waterproof coating, the final layer of protection should be a dimpled membrane. This is the best solution I know of to prevent water infiltration in a basement. You've probably seen rolls of this dimpled membrane in building stores, or on the foundations of new homes under construction. It gets rolled out against the exterior foundation wall, and then is mechanically fastened to it with fasteners that self-seal. In fact, this type of dimpled membrane is all that's required by the building code as a foundation wrap, but I like to go the extra step of applying a waterproofing membrane first, as described above.

The dimpled membrane makes sure that groundwater will never be in contact with the foundation wall, and more importantly it eases hydrostatic pressure build-up against your foundation. The dimples in the membrane create an air gap at the foundation wall, which allows the wall to breathe and eliminates any headwater pressure against the wall. Any groundwater that gets past the membrane will drain to the footings and be taken away by the weeping tiles.

Once the dimpled membrane is fastened to the wall, the trench around the foundation should be backfilled and tamped down. The top edge of the membrane shouldn't be covered over or caulked; there should be at least 1 inch of the membrane above grade. Expect that some of the topsoil may settle unevenly around the foundation about six months to a year after the job is done, since it's impossible for backfilling to give you the same soil compactness that existed before. It's more than a matter of looks, since proper drainage around your foundation can only happen if there's the correct degree of slope away from the foundation walls.

The sump pump drainage system—
getting the water away from your house

The last part of any waterproofing system is the installation of a sump pump drainage system. This system consists of a sump pump, a sump well, and a discharge pipe. The sump well is basically a hole in your basement floor that collects water from the weeping tiles. The sump pump then pumps the water out and away from the house via a discharge pipe.

A critical part of your waterproofing system, the sump pump collects water from your weeping tile and pumps it away from your house.

There are different types of sump pumps. A pedestal pump is located above the water level and uses a float switch to activate the pump when water levels rise. A submersible pump also uses a float switch to activate the pump, but it's submerged in the sump pit so that it's out of sight and out of earshot. This is great if you're using your basement as living space, but keep in mind its life span is shorter than a pedestal pump because of the simple fact that it sits in water all the time.

For backup (when the electricity fails), water-powered or battery-powered sump pumps are a wise form of additional insurance against flooding.

There are a few things to look for when choosing a sump pump:

- **non-corrosive materials, especially for submersible sump pumps**
- **horsepower—most pumps range from ⅙ to ½ HP**
- **gallons per hour the pump will move**

This last point will depend on your situation. If your basement floods a lot every spring, you're going to want a heavy-duty pump that can handle the flow.

After the pump, your next big concern should be drainage of the pump. I see a lot of sump pumps draining water outside, right next to the foundation wall—which is just pointless. The water you've just pumped out of your basement works its way right back in. For your system to work, the water has to drain several metres away from your foundation wall—and from any other building, such as your neighbour's house.

Assessing your drains

Another serious source of basement water damage is a sewer backup. Before you have your basement finished, make sure the drains are reliable. Otherwise, you could spend your hard-earned money on a beautifully finished basement—and find everything destroyed when the next storm hits.

Every drain in your house—sinks, toilets, showers, and laundry—goes to the main stack that runs under your basement floor. The stack leads to the sanitary sewer line in the street, and then eventually to your city's sewer system.

A sewer backup can be caused by a blockage in your drain, and the solution is simple: call a plumber to come and clear it out. In older houses, sometimes the backup is caused by old-style clay pipe breaking down with age. Sometimes tree roots can wrap themselves around the pipe and break it or get inside and block the pipe so water can't flow, which will cause a backup of sewage into your house.

If you have an old, clay tile drain, have a camera inspection done by a professional. Make sure the inspector puts a time stamp on the video, notes at what distance from the house any potential obstructions are located, and has a copy of the video made for you to keep on file. If the sewer backs up after a heavy downpour and

The first step in any renovation should be to have your drains inspected for any problems. You don't want a backup to wreck your newly renovated basement.

the city drains are at fault, you'll have a record of your drain's condition prior to the storm, which could help you get compensation for any damage.

If there's a problem with your clay tile drain, get it replaced with PVC before you have another backup. Do this before you finish that basement! Yes, you'll have to excavate, and the contractor might have to break up your basement floor to do the job right, but it will be money well spent.

If the drain looks good, I would check it again in two or three years. If it looks like there are breaks in the tile and a tree root or dirt is getting into the drain, but there's still no significant danger, check it again next year. But whatever you do, don't spend money on any finishes to your basement without making sure your drains are in good shape first.

In new homes, the storm drains and sewers are separate, so you don't have storm water overloading the municipal system and backing sewage into your home. But you can still end up with a sewer flood if there's a blockage downstream, either on your property or in the general municipal system.

A sewer drain can also back up into your house when the back pressure from the main line in the street is so great—a major storm is the most likely culprit—that the water can't be handled by the system. The water gets forced back up your main sanitary sewer pipe and into your home.

One way to stop that from happening is to have a professional install a backflow preventer inside the house in the main drain, under the concrete floor ahead of the cleanout.

Some homebuilders now install them as standard on new homes, but backflow preventers are actually not legal in some municipalities. The city's thinking is that, if everyone gets a backflow preventer, the pressure from a backup with nowhere to go may destroy its sewer system. In other words, the city prefers to use your house as a handy pressure relief valve, whether it costs you the destruction of your basement or not.

If it's legal in your municipality, I recommend having a backflow preventer installed before finishing your basement. It could save the basement from disaster, and in the meantime it could also mean a reduction in your insurance premium.

Insulation

I'll tell you what I've learned from more than 30 years in the building trade. I've seen basements that were insulated according to code and they failed miserably. I've seen just about every theory out there—including the idea that you don't have to insulate any part of the wall that's below grade—and I know that every one of them can lead to big problems with moisture and mould in the long run. I've seen these basements because I've been called in to fix them.

Two things you don't want to see: the dirt on the left edge of the batt insulation is a sign of air movement, and the dark wood below is a sign of water damage.

If you think that moisture and mould don't sound too serious, think again: not only will they likely cause every surface in your basement to rot, they can also rot the wooden structural components of your house, and cause serious health problems to anyone living in the house, particularly children and older people. Mould also smells bad—it's that musty smell I'm sure you're familiar with—and it won't make you look forward to spending time in that lavishly finished basement. Might as well kiss your investment goodbye.

Why is a poorly insulated basement the perfect environment for mould to thrive? Most people think about insulation as important because it keeps the basement warm in winter, and that's true. But it's even more important in the summer, when heat and humidity can cause a lot of moisture to build up.

Because basements are mostly underground, they have a unique situation with regard to air temperature. At the basement floor level—many feet below grade—the temperature remains fairly constant, just like the soil outside your foundation walls.

But as you go up towards the ceiling, the temperature will rise. The air temperature near the ceiling of your basement is always higher than at floor level. So what's the big deal with that?

The big deal is that once you've finished your basement (if you haven't insulated properly), warm air from inside your nice new drywall will come into contact with the foundation walls behind the insulation. Warm air holds moisture, and this moisture will condense when the air cools as it comes into contact with the cold exterior wall. This moisture will collect in your insulation and in your wood framing, and will even pool at floor level behind your finished walls. Mould spores will flourish.

And, no matter what, if you insulate your basement the same way you do an above-grade wall—using wood studs against the wall, with batt insulation in between and a vapour barrier over that—you'll have air movement and problems with condensation and, very likely, with mould.

What I recommend is using rigid foam insulation against all the outside walls and the floor. Use it 2 inches thick on the walls and 1 inch thick on the floor. (See more about basement flooring on pages 48 and 49.) This foam comes shiplapped, so each piece fits snugly against the next with no gaps. All rigid foam insulation is mould- and mildew-resistant and won't hold moisture, even if you have a flood in your basement.

Make sure each seam is Tuck-taped and use spray foam to fill any gaps around the edges.

When finishing a basement, you want a thermal break on the exterior walls. Rigid foam stops air movement behind the walls, which leads to condensation and mould.

Then, you can put up studs in front of the foam and finish your basement. What you've done is create a thermal break between the air inside your basement and the air outside, eliminating any air movement behind the walls that leads to condensation.

Spray foam insulation is similar to rigid foam insulation, but it's applied on-site in spray form. It's an even better solution than rigid foam because it creates intimate contact with the walls, and it doesn't allow any moisture or air movement. If your contractor is going to use spray foam, make sure the studs are built with space behind them so they won't come in direct contact with the concrete walls. This way the foam will be able to reach behind them.

With either spray foam or rigid foam, you can think of the effect as being like a beer cooler. Beer coolers are made with rigid foam insulation between the layers of plastic. It might be a hot sunny day at the beach, but inside the cooler your beer stays cold and ice doesn't melt. And there's no dripping condensation on the outside of your cooler either—that's what the thermal break prevents. It's the same with newer toilet tanks—they all come lined with rigid foam to stop the annoying drip of condensation you used to get on old toilet tanks, caused by the cold water inside the tank meeting the warm air of the bathroom.

If you use this method, you'll be free to choose any finishing materials at all—you won't have to worry about how moisture will affect them because your basement will be as dry as if it were above grade. You can rest assured that your drywall will remain dry, and that other investments you make in the basement will last for many years.

Moisture from basement floors

As you're probably realizing, moisture is a huge issue in the basement, more so than anywhere else in your house. I want to talk more about the basement floor, and how important it is to prepare it properly before finishing it. We've just discussed the issue of condensation that happens below ground, but what about the water that's right under your house?

Under every house, there's water somewhere. The question is, how far down is it? The highest point at which the soil is saturated is what's called the water table. If you were able to dig down far enough under your house, you'd see groundwater, not just damp soil, and that would be your water table. The water table could be just under the surface, and its level can change depending on the season and the weather patterns.

Basement floors can actually be on or very close to the water table, and of course that can be challenging. Most houses, whether they were built fifty years ago or five, have basement floors made of concrete. Newer houses are likely to have about 4 inches of gravel under the concrete, which provides a bit of drainage. Really old houses might have only a thin layer of concrete, with no gravel underneath, and the oldest houses might have only a dirt floor. But no matter how much gravel is under the concrete, or how thick the concrete is, moisture can and will travel through the concrete and into the floor.

Most often, you're going to see people finishing their basement floor as if moisture wasn't even an issue, and I suppose for a few years you might not notice a real problem. You'll see vinyl, tile, or linoleum—and even hardwood—laid right on the concrete floor. Sometimes you'll hear people say that they've put down a 6-mil plastic sheet vapour barrier before applying the finish flooring. In fact, that's what the building code recommends.

I think that's a big mistake. By putting down any kind of vapour barrier, you're just trapping the moisture from the concrete, which is sure to form mould. You won't be able to see the mould, but you'll probably smell it, and you'll definitely be breathing it in—which isn't good for anybody's health.

If you use an epoxy-based product, or oil-based paint, or any other kind of sealer on concrete, you're also just going to trap the moisture, and the pressure that builds up from the water underneath is going to cause the sealer to fail.

The better way is to have your contractor put down a layer of 1" rigid foam board insulation over the concrete. Rigid foam creates a thermal break and provides a moisture barrier. But make sure your contractor doesn't glue the boards down. This is an important point, since organic materials like mastic and some glues applied directly to a concrete floor can lead to mould growth. Glue is the perfect food source for mould spores. So, no glue.

Instead, use low-expansion spray foam along all the exterior edges, where the flooring meets the walls, and then Tuck-tape every joint. On top of the foam you need a layer of ⅝" tongue-and-groove plywood, which should be screwed through the foam and into the concrete floor using Tapcon screws. They're designed for concrete, and they're the best on the market.

Once you've got this base, you can put down any type of flooring you want, even hardwood. If you're thinking of tile of any kind, I'd still use a Schluter-Ditra membrane as a base because it will cushion the tile, but any other kind of flooring can go directly over that base. It's strong and stable, and it's not going to let moisture through.

Adding these layers to the floor is going to steal some headroom from your basement—about 1½ inches—so you need to account for this. Most modern basements will have plenty of room for this, but if you're going to the trouble of lowering your basement floor, you want to make sure you go low enough. That's why I say you should allow at least 2½ inches in your calculations for subflooring, finish flooring, and ceiling finishes.

With a proper base on your floor, you'll have your pick of floor coverings. Even if you use carpeting, you'll avoid the musty carpet smell that's common in many basement renos.

Basement insulation in new homes

You might think that some of the previous stuff I've said about insulating your basement only counts for people with older homes. If you've got a new house, you've probably only got insulation and a vapour barrier over the top part of your basement walls—the part that's above the frost line. That's because builders today are required to insulate only that top portion. And because they only have to use batt insulation covered by a plastic vapour barrier, there's a thermal "barrier" but no thermal break. That means cold and hot can still meet, especially on the bottom edge of the plastic sheet.

Batt insulation won't stop condensation. Condensation occurs when cool air comes in contact with a warm surface, or vice versa. Either warm moist air in the house contacts a cooler basement wall or floor, or cool air-conditioned air contacts a warmer wall, perhaps one above grade.

You need a thermal break with a vapour barrier to completely separate interior conditioned air from exterior air. (We say "conditioned" because that means it's either warmed in winter or cooled in summer. It's not the same as the exterior air.)

The downside of vapour barriers is that they don't allow your home to breathe because now the house is essentially shrouded in plastic. Naturally occurring humidity and moisture from our skin, our breath, cooking, bathing, and indoor plants have nowhere to go, and if enough moisture is trapped, it will accumulate on the inside of that plastic barrier. Not good.

Condensation happens most during the hottest and coldest months of the year. In the winter, the exposed part of the foundation wall is cold in comparison to the heated air from the furnace that comes in contact with it, which creates condensation. In the summer the reverse happens, especially when your air conditioning is on. Cool air sinks to the basement and makes contact with the basement walls (that are now warm, in comparison). Again, this creates condensation.

With exterior basement walls that are only half-insulated and half-covered in a vapour barrier, it's difficult to create an airtight seal on the bottom edge where the plastic sheet meets the concrete wall. So then moisture forms on the inside surface of the plastic sheet and soaks the insulation, and water drips out the bottom.

A little bit of moisture is not so much the concern. However, the moisture becomes a bigger problem when there's a constant source of moisture, since mould loves to grow in this type of environment.

Is this a bad situation? I would say so. Do the writers behind the building code think this is a serious situation? Apparently not. In fact, just over a decade ago the Ontario Building Code took a giant step backwards. In houses built before 1996, a device called a heat recovery ventilator (HRV) was a mandatory requirement. This device exchanges air from inside the house with outside air. It's a good solution for controlling moisture in airtight homes, and every new home should have one—but now they don't.

I recommend that owners of new homes—anyone who has purchased a newly built home since 1996—do two things. One, replace the half-cocked, minimum-code insulation job with a proper thermal break (such as spray foam or rigid foam insulation) that completely covers the basement walls at the very least. And two, install an HRV to help control the overall moisture levels in their home, and help limit the potential for mould growth.

In fact, every homeowner should have an HRV installed. It should be ducted on its own to allow fresh air to come in from the outside, and to accommodate a HEPA filter that removes 99.9% of impurities—including mould spores and dust—from the air. If you can't manage that, make sure you have a high-efficiency furnace that is ducted to the outside to bring fresh air in.

Once these concerns are dealt with, you'll have moisture problems under control, and you can proceed with finishing the basement correctly.

Waterproofing and insulating the attic

In an attic that's structurally suitable for conversion to living space, you need to address the possibility of water and moisture before you insulate or finish the space.

If the attic isn't finished yet at all, you're probably looking at raw wood—the underside of your roof. Take a close look at the wood to determine if there's water damage from leaks over the years. Odds are, with an older house that was built using rafters, you're going to see water stains. The question is, are those stains due to current leaks, or have the leaks been taken care of by a recent roofing job?

If moisture is making its way through the roof and into your existing unfinished attic, it may take you a while to notice the problem. At no time do you want rain or snow to penetrate the roof and damage the inside of your house, but this is especially true if you're planning to finish the attic. Make sure you get a thorough inspection of your roof first, and be sure that all the components of the roofing system—including the shingles, flashing, underlayment, roof decking, soffits, and fascia—are in perfect working order.

Depending on what kind of roof you have, it may actually be preferable to find that you're in need of a new roof at the same time as you're converting the attic to living space. Why? Because the best way to insulate and seal the attic is with a spray foam polyurethane insulation, such as Walltite Eco, and the best roof above that is a metal roof.

Let's go back a few steps.

Although it might look as though attics are just wasted space, they actually serve an important function. That empty space is a "cold zone," a breathable area that prevents moisture from building up on the roof. Moisture is created whenever warm air meets cool air. If your attic isn't properly sealed off from the rest of the house, during the winter a lot of warm air will escape into the attic (remember that cold air always pushes hot) and cause condensation to collect. That will mean some serious ice dams on the roof that will get under your shingles and shorten their lifespan. The attic is the buffer zone that prevents this from happening.

Now, if we remove that breathable buffer zone by finishing the attic, we've got a ceiling that's only inches away from the roof. Most building codes tell you that in order to prevent moisture problems in a situation like this, you should make sure your rafters allow enough space for standard 10" fibreglass batt insulation (with an R-value of 30), plus a 2" ventilation space that's created by installing a ventilation baffle. If the rafters aren't at least 12 inches deep, furring strips must be added to make them deep enough for both the insulation and the ventilation baffle. A plastic vapour barrier is then installed (on the warm side), and then ½" drywall is used to finish the ceiling.

Sounds good, doesn't it? The problem is it doesn't work. I've seen this system fail again and again. It's not possible to get enough ventilation. So condensation is

The attic is a cold zone, so you want proper insulation in the ceiling to keep the rest of the house warm in the winter. Here, the mix of loose and batt insulation is not deep enough to do the job.

inevitable with this system. Sometimes you see it on the surface of the roof, in the form of ice dams, and sometimes you see it on the inside, with water condensing and dripping from the ceiling. Sometimes you're "lucky" enough to get both.

The better option is to create a complete thermal break between hot and cold, just as I suggested you do with basement walls and floors. You need an insulator that will actually keep hot and cold from coming into contact with one another. That way, there's no opportunity for moisture to condense. The only insulation that does that adequately is a closed-cell polyurethane foam, which would be sprayed onto the exposed rafters and the underside of the roof decking.

To completely stop any thermal bridging (transfer of heat or cold) through the wooden rafters, a layer of 2" rigid foam insulation should also be applied over the entire area, and then finished with ½" drywall. Use the same system on any dormers that you add, to prevent problems with moisture or condensation.

Let me say a little bit more about why I like closed-cell polyurethane insulation. It fills every crevice and acts as its own vapour barrier when it's applied in a thickness of at least 2 inches. It deters insects and provides more R-value in the same space than any other insulation. And it can only be installed by licensed contractors, so you have some assurance that the work will be done properly and recourse if it's not.

But make sure you are getting closed-cell foam, not open-cell. There's a big difference. Open-cell is softer, relies on air for insulation, and provides less R-value. It's lighter, at between ½ and ¾ pounds per cubic foot, whereas closed-cell is between 2 and 3 pounds per cubic foot. Open-cell is cheaper per cubic foot and per unit of

Closed-cell spray foam is your best bet for insulation. It fills every crevice and forms a thermal break that stops air movement and prevents moisture and condensation.

R-value, but its effectiveness is reduced if it gets wet so it needs a separate application of vapour barrier.

A better roof

There's only one drawback to closed-cell foam insulation. When foam insulation is applied directly to the underside of the roof, it traps the roof deck (sheathing) between the insulation and the asphalt shingles. The sheathing no longer "breathes," and it overheats the shingles on hot days. That's a problem, because when asphalt shingles get too hot, they break down more quickly and don't have the lifespan they should. The sheathing is also damaged by high heat, so you have a problem on your hands.

The solution is a better roof. In my view, asphalt shingles aren't the way to go anymore. Far better to use the spray foam insulation and replace your aging asphalt roof with a long-lasting metal roof—or at least know that you'll upgrade to a metal roof when the time comes to replace the asphalt.

Make sure the old roof is stripped down to the plywood sheathing, and that any rotten sheathing is replaced. Stay away from tarpaper as an underlayment, since it will break down, and use a good ice and water shield in valleys and gutters. Use a synthetic roof paper called Grace Tri-Flex Xtreme over top of your ice and water shield, all over the roof. It's waterproof, it's guaranteed for six months even without a roof, and it's non-slip wet or dry. That's a bonus for the roofers, since it's skid-resistant even in steep slope applications. It's not cheap, but it's much better than standard tarpaper in quality.

Then, have the roof strapped—first vertically, then horizontally—before the metal shingles or panels are applied. This way, you're creating an air space above the sheathing that will allow it to breathe. A metal roof is more expensive than a traditional asphalt roof, but it's a much better investment in the long run: it's going to have a fifty-year guarantee; it's going to perform better against rain, wind, and sun; and it's fire-rated, so your house is more likely to be unharmed if a neighbouring house catches fire.

Another option, if you're really ambitious, is to go the whole way and replace your asphalt shingles with a green roof. The technologies for green roofs have come a long way in a few short years, and there are now green roof applications for flat as well as sloping roofs. You have to make sure your structure can support the additional weight load of a green roof, but the environmental and economic benefits could definitely make it worth your while.

Following up: Checklist for attic structure, waterproofing, and insulation

❏ **Is your house built using traditional rafters or modern-day trusses? If you see trusses in the attic, it's probably best to look elsewhere in your house for extra space.**

❏ **What's the load-bearing capacity of your attic floor? Consult a structural engineer to determine this.**

❏ **Is there any type of staircase to the attic? If yes, are the dimensions safe? If not, where can a staircase be installed?**

❏ **Is the full-height area of the attic adequate for satisfying the building code specifications for living space? If not, can dormer windows be used to increase living space?**

❏ **Does the attic have adequate light and air, with operable windows? At least one window must meet code criteria as a fire escape. Ensure that any new or enlarged windows are well supported above and below, and do not compromise structure.**

❏ **Are there signs of water damage or wetness anywhere in the attic? Identify any sources of water or moisture penetration.**

❏ **Is there adequate insulation? My preference is "intimate contact" insulation, such as closed-cell polyurethane, on attic ceilings, rafters, and knee walls. Cover the entire area, including rafters, with 2" rigid foam insulation, then finish with ½" drywall.**

❏ **Is your roof compatible with a properly insulated attic? If not, consider replacing your asphalt shingled roof with a metal roof or green roof or plan to do so in the near future.**

Following up:
Checklist for basement structure, waterproofing, and insulation

❑ Is there adequate headroom in the basement for living space—at least 90 inches, plus at least 2½ inches for flooring insulation, finish flooring, and a ceiling? If not, your options are underpinning or bench-pinning the basement to gain headroom. If you're underpinning, use this as an opportunity to address waterproofing and drainage issues from the exterior.

❑ Do you need additional or enlarged windows and/or doors? If so, ensure these are adequately framed and supported, and deal with exterior waterproofing and drainage issues as the work is done.

❑ Does your design plan require moving or removing any interior walls or structural supports? If so, consult a structural engineer before you remove anything.

❑ Are there signs of water or moisture in the basement? Identify all sources of water and moisture.

❑ Is the foundation exterior adequately protected from water and moisture? An ideal exterior drainage system includes a series of waterproofing membranes, as well as weeping tile and a sump pump system.

❑ Is the basement fully insulated, floor to ceiling, to create a thermal break with high R-values? The system I recommend includes 2" rigid foam board on walls, 1" rigid foam on floors, and a top-quality form of "intimate contact" insulation, such as closed-cell polyurethane (Walltite) over studs and wiring.

❑ Does your basement have an HRV with direct ducting to the outside and a HEPA filter to remove air impurities? If not, have a high-quality system installed to ensure good air quality.

CHAPTER 3

Electrical, Plumbing, and HVAC

Turning a basement or attic into finished space means changing the way you use those spaces. You'll need good lighting, a comfortable temperature year-round, and you might need plumbing that didn't exist before. Doing this will require a lot of changes to the mechanical systems in your house—the electrical, plumbing, and HVAC (heating, ventilation, and air conditioning). It's easy to get these changes wrong, and disturb systems that might have worked just fine before you started. Let's go through each one of these systems so you can understand how they work, and how they might they need to be updated, improved, replaced, or added onto during the course of your basement or attic reno.

Electrical

First things first: When it comes to electrical work, don't even think about doing it yourself. I don't do my own electrical work, and neither should you or anyone else who isn't an electrician. There's no point in risking your life while you're working on the electrical, or taking a chance that your lack of expertise could cause a house fire someday that would rob you of your possessions or even your life.

Put safety at the top of the list

When you hire a licensed, experienced electrician, you'll see that safety is their first priority too—their safety as they work, and your safety as you live in that house. A good electrician will warn you if there are safety issues that have to be addressed in your electrical panel, or in other wiring they see in your house. Safety is usually more of an issue in older homes, or in houses that have already been "improved" a lot over the years, but it can also crop up as a problem in newer houses.

As soon as an electrician opens up your electrical panel, he'll be able to tell a lot about the wiring in your house. How large is the service and can it support more circuits? How old is the wiring and what kind is it? Is it original wiring or was the house rewired at some point? Most importantly, has the wiring been done correctly?

Dealing with unexpected wiring issues will cost you money. It can derail your other reno plans if your budget isn't flexible enough to deal with contingencies like this. That's why it's important to have a licensed electrician take a look at your panel and your wiring before you finalize your renovation plans, so you'll be sure about what you're already dealing with.

Let's look at the important questions that you should ask your electrician as you're planning your renovation.

How large is the service and can it support more circuits?

The wiring in your house carries 120 volts. But voltage won't tell you how much electricity is actually moving through a wire. That's amperage. Fuses and circuit breakers are rated in amperage. It's amperage you should be concerned about, because it's amps we talk about when we refer to the heart of the electrical system in your house: the main service panel.

The wiring in your house is just a collection of circuits that are routed through the main service panel. The panel brings the raw electricity into the house from the municipal lines (you'll see a heavy cable inside the box), and converts it into electricity that can be used for appliances, lights, etc.

There's a fuse or a circuit breaker for every circuit. Each circuit will be rated for a maximum amperage, usually 15 amps, and that circuit shouldn't be overloaded. A good rule of thumb is that you should have no more than 12 devices per 15-amp circuit. (A device can be anything from a switch receptacle to a light.)

The main service panel in older houses is often a fuse box. In newer systems, it's a panel of circuit breakers. Both work the same way. When you ask for too much electric current through a circuit by plugging in too many appliances, the fuse will burn out, or the circuit breaker will cut the connection. In this way the wire is kept from overheating and causing a fire.

If you have a 60-amp service to your house, it's not enough. You'll need 100 amps for sure, but you might consider upgrading to 200 amps, depending on your plans for

The first stop in an electrical inspection is your panel. Here, an electrician can spot potential red flags.

the future. If you have a lot of appliances, electronic equipment, or electric in-floor heating, or any plans to divide your home into separate living units, a 200-amp service is likely the way to go.

It can be difficult to tell how large the service is at your house, since circuit panels are hard to decipher and the outside meter might or might not be correct. Rely on a licensed electrician for a definitive answer. Then discuss your renovation plans with the electrician so they can help you determine if the electrical service will need to be expanded to accommodate everything safely.

How old is the wiring and what kind is it?

Depending on the age of your home, and any renovations that may already have been done, you're likely to find one, or even all three types of wiring: knob and tube, aluminum, or copper.

The earliest kind of wiring was knob and tube, and it was installed up until about 1945. Knob-and-tube wiring was safe enough when it was first used, and would be still today except we live in an electronic age and everything needs power. Not a problem, 70 to 80 years ago, but people began using power bars and loading up the supply line, causing it to get hot and increasing the chance of a fire. That's why today's minimum code—along with most insurance companies—requires that knob and tube be replaced.

Aluminum wiring had a brief burst of popularity in the 1960s and 1970s. It was a good innovation at the time, but the move to copper wiring has meant that a lot of houses with aluminum wiring ended up, over the years, with a mix of copper and aluminum. Just like with knob and tube, it was mixing the different types of wires that caused problems. For an aluminum system to be safe, it must be all aluminum— panel, receptacles, switches, lighting. That's not very practical anymore, when the standard now is copper.

The third and most common type of wiring you'll find in any house built since the late 1970s is copper. It's the industry standard, and by far the best conductor available.

Is it original wiring or was the house rewired at some point?
Most importantly, has the wiring been done correctly?

As with structure, most houses start out with wiring that's done properly and safely. Over the years, though, as people make changes, there's the possibility that ignorance or sloppy workmanship can lead to errors. Those errors can be costly to fix, but with electrical it's extremely important that you do fix them.

When you bring in an electrician to check out your current system, ask about the quality of any work that's visible. They can tell a lot just by looking at the main panel. If you're starting with raw, unfinished space in the basement or attic, that's a good thing, because it means that a lot of your electrical will already be exposed and easy to judge. And doing the electrical, plumbing, and HVAC will be far easier in the basement than in an attic because the basement is where the systems start.

If your whole house has wiring issues . . .

If your house has wiring that dates before the 1970s (either knob and tube or aluminum), or if there are visible safety issues, your electrician may suggest major upgrades or even wholesale replacement. This may be a lot more than you bargained for—or budgeted for.

Electrical cable should be run through joists, not underneath them.

If you can't afford to replace the entire system at once, consider doing it in stages. These should be your priorities:

- **Start by dealing with immediate safety concerns.**
- **Upgrade the service panel to an appropriate amperage level (at least 100 amps, and maybe more).**
- **For renovated areas, have all-new copper wiring installed for any electrical need. New wiring should be run directly back to the panel, not tied into older wiring elsewhere in the house.**
- **Upgrade wiring to other rooms later, as you can afford it.**

In the long run, you may spend a bit more to rewire your house this way, but this may fit your budget better than trying to do a whole-house electrical job along with the changes you're making to your basement or attic.

Planning for electrical

Electrical needs, of course, are closely tied to the overall design of the space you want to renovate or convert, because you're looking at lighting, receptacles, and maybe appliances such as an extra kitchen range. Electrical wiring and other types of wiring go behind the walls, so you've got to think ten steps ahead. It can be tough to imagine exactly how you'll use your new space, but the more you can do that, the better your renovation.

Here are some points to help you determine what you need for electrical:

- **Consider whether any lights or receptacles should run on three-way switches. Three-ways allow you to flip the switch from more than one location, which is particularly useful at different entrances to the same room, or at the top and bottom of stairs. It's important for both safety and convenience.**
- **If the room will be used as a bedroom, have outlets installed on either side of where the bed is likely to be positioned—where bedside tables will be placed—but away from the bed itself. If you're absolutely certain of the location of the bed, consider having wall sconces hardwired into place on either side of the bed.**
- **For convenience, use a three-way switch for the overhead light in a bedroom, with one switch near the entrance to the room, and others near bedside tables.**
- **Any bedroom outlets should be AFCIs—arc fault circuit interrupters. These are important safety features that could prevent serious fires and are required by code in many areas in North America.**

MIKE'S TIP

Watch for these electrical red flags.

Here are some signs that a handyperson decided to take on the electrical work instead of hiring a licensed electrician:

- Wiring has been run underneath joists instead of through them. Any wiring that runs along the underside of a joist could be punctured by a drywall screw or nail at some point, and that's a real danger.
- Junction boxes are hidden behind walls or concealed in some way. Whenever wires are joined up, they should be enclosed in a proper metal junction box, and that junction box must be clearly visible and accessible, even after the finishing work is done.
- Wires are joined together with electrical tape rather than in a junction box. This is a fire waiting to happen.
- Ceiling joists and/or wall studs have been "notched" out to make room for wiring. This compromises the strength of the framing and should never be done. Wires should only be run through small holes drilled through the centre of the joists or studs.
- Wires are hanging loose inside the wall cavity, instead of stapled to joists or studs. By code, wires must be stapled to the joist or stud within 16 inches of any electrical box.
- Coloured wires are visible just outside an electrical box. All coloured wires should be enclosed in white plastic sheathing, and at least a ¼ inch of the sheathing should be inside the electrical box—therefore, no coloured wires should be visible.

- Any outlet that's within 6 feet of a water source must be a GFCI—ground fault circuit interrupter. This type of outlet cuts the power current if water comes in contact with the outlet.
- Electrical codes require that no point along any wall should be more than 6 feet from an electrical outlet. This is meant to discourage the use of extension cords.
- Ask yourself what kind of wiring you might need in the future for telephones, televisions, stereo speakers, or computer equipment. I recommend running some 1½" ABS piping right through the house (on all exterior and interior walls) so that you'll be able to fish any type of wiring through it in the future without breaking up the walls. Make a map of where the ABS is so you can access it easily later.

- Consider your lighting needs carefully, and plan accordingly. (See more in the section on lighting below.)

- In closets, have an overhead light installed inside with an automatic shut-off switch to prevent fires. You won't regret the added expense.

- If ceiling fans are part of your plans (especially useful with high-ceilinged rooms, which may be the case in an attic), make sure your electrician knows if you want the fan and light to operate on separate switches. Special wiring and framing are needed for ceiling fans.

- If electrical in-floor radiant heat is part of your heating plan, make sure your electrician knows this ahead of time so they can provide the necessary wiring. It has to be wired directly to the electrical panel, on a dedicated circuit.

- If you're planning a bathroom in the basement or attic, you'll need ventilation. Decide where your exhaust fan will be placed, and whether it will function together with a light or on a separate switch.

- New electrical standards in Canada require the use of outlets that have a "shutter" that closes down when something is inserted into only one prong. The outlet will only work when both prongs are penetrated. This new regulation is meant to prevent children from being electrocuted by pushing things into outlets.

- Another new standard in Canada is the requirement that every home have a hard-wired carbon monoxide detector. A battery-run detector that can wear down won't be good enough anymore.

A closer look at lighting

Any lighting plan should include both natural light—meaning windows or sky-lights—and artificial light. Your lighting plan should be extensive enough to give you adequate light for day and night, and flexible enough to achieve different needs.

Artificial light is usually divided into three categories: general or ambient lighting (usually these are overhead lights), task lighting (brighter lights used over a work space), and accent lighting (such as pot lights around the perimeter of the room, wall sconces, and lamps).

Start by determining how much artificial light you'll need to light the room at night. A general guideline is to take the square footage of the room and multiply it by 1.5: this will give you the wattage needed to light the room to full brightness with a regular incandescent light. As an example, a room that's 10 feet by 12 feet is 120 square feet. Multiplied by 1.5, that's 180. So you'd need approximately 180 watts of light in total to illuminate the room with incandescent light. LED and

Make the switch to LED lights.

Mention energy-efficient lighting and most people think of compact fluorescent lamps, or CFL. They might also change the subject, because CFL lights have their drawbacks. They contain mercury, they take time to reach full brightness, their flickering can be annoying, and the quality of light they give isn't to everyone's taste.

There's another option: light-emitting diodes, or LED. You've seen them for years in the digital display on your alarm clock, the tail lights of your car, or in strings of Christmas tree lights. And they're being used more and more around the house.

LED lights are even more energy efficient than CFL, and they last longer, too—roughly ten times as long as CFL, and between 50 and 100 times as long as an incandescent bulb.

Unlike incandescent lights, which use electric current to heat a filament to the point that it glows and gives off light (and lots of heat), LED lights pass electricity through a semiconductor material. More than 80% of the energy is turned into light, while generating next to no heat.

Because LED light is highly directional—that is, it shines where it's pointed, whereas other types scatter in all directions—it has traditionally been used for task lighting. In kitchens, LED fixtures are excellent over work spaces like the stove, sink, or island. They're also a very good choice for accent lighting, installed under the cabinets.

LED lights are also being used more and more for mood lighting. There are new products that are ideal for cove lighting, and are even dimmable.

The technology does have drawbacks. You may find the light too cold or too intense—LED lights don't provide that yellowish glow you get from incandescent bulbs. And they're certainly more expensive to buy, although prices are coming down, and you come out ahead on the electricity you save—they pay for themselves in a couple of years.

I've used LED lights on many projects, including in my own home. They're worth looking into as you plan your renovation.

flourescent lights use less wattage, but generally have an equivalent number for incandescent light.

That number is a minimum. You'll probably want more than that, from a number of different sources, to give your lighting design lots of flexibility. Think about where you want ceiling lights, floor lamps, table lamps, and any lights for built-ins or other display areas where you want to have focussed accent lighting.

Recessed lighting is a common choice for basements. If you are adding soundproof insulation in your ceiling, be sure that the lighting fixtures are designated as IC (in contact) so they can be installed next to insulation.

You see a lot of additional living space divided into rooms. But how is each area heated and cooled? Is the air moving well throughout the basement? Was an HVAC specialist consulted?

You see a great-looking bar with a sink. How is the sink installed? If it's not properly vented, the drain won't work well.

It might look like a high-end renovation with a lot of expensive details and finishes, but it's lipstick and mascara to me. I'd want to know if the rest of the renovation is just as good. For example, is there a proper thermal break on the floor so the carpet stays dry?

What you see.
What I see.

Multiple lighting sources are always good, though I'm not sure you need the lights in the stairs. It could be annoying to replace the bulbs here, so I'd like to see long-lasting and efficient LEDs.

Designing with recessed lighting

Recessed lighting is versatile—it gives great overall illumination to a room as well as task lighting where it's needed, and it doesn't take up headroom in low-ceilinged areas like basements. You can even use a recessed light in a shower if you use the correct type for a wet zone.

Here are some things to know if you're planning to use recessed lighting in your basement or attic renovation:

- **Using recessed lights around the perimeter of a small room will make the space feel larger.**
- **Use this simple rule to determine how close together the lights should be installed: 4" fixtures should be placed at least 4 feet apart and 6" fixtures about 6 feet apart.**
- **If you want to spotlight a feature of your room like art, centre the fixtures in front of the objects to be lit—and about 12 to 18 inches in front of the objects.**
- **To light a three-dimensional object such as a fireplace or sculpture, use at least two or three lights so the object is being lit from several angles.**
- **Choose recessed reflectors when you want the most light from a fixture, or install white or black baffle trims to focus and direct light or reduce glare.**

Recessed lighting—installing it right

Recessed lighting has to be properly installed. With the wrong type of fixture for the job, or too many fixtures on a circuit, you could have an accident waiting to happen.

Most light bulbs—with the exception of LED lights—generate heat, especially incandescent or halogen bulbs. That's not a big deal in a table or floor lamp, since they are used in well-ventilated areas. But in a recessed light, which is tucked into a floor or ceiling cavity, that heat needs to escape, or the fixture will overheat and a fire could start.

There are two basic types of pot lights: those designed for areas that won't come into contact with insulation, and those for areas that will. It's critical that you use the right type.

According to code, only recessed lights designated IC (for "in contact") can be installed directly next to insulation. They have a rectangular metal box around them that creates an air space between the fixture and any insulation so they won't overheat.

One place I don't like using recessed lights is in ceilings below a cold zone. A cold zone could be an attic space, or any area directly below the roof. If you're finishing

Recessed lighting is a common choice for basements. If you are adding soundproof insulation in your ceiling, be sure that the lighting fixtures are designated as IC (in contact) so they can be installed next to insulation.

your attic with any method that requires ventilation between the roof and the insulation, you've still got a cold zone there.

The air temperature in a cold zone should be about the same as outside. But if you've got a recessed light fixture—or several—in that space, you're going to get some heat rising into that cold zone. And because pot lights aren't perfectly sealed (they have small holes in them to allow warm air to escape), they'll let warm air from the room below into the cold zone. You don't want any source of heat in a cold zone.

Why not? Because when that heat meets the air in the cold zone, it will lead to condensation, which can cause water damage on the ceiling below, and can also promote the growth of mould. The heat loss can also melt the snow cover on your roof from below, which will then freeze again when the lights go off. Eventually an ice dam will form—and that's not good for your roof.

If you really want recessed lighting in your finished attic—no matter what kind of insulation you're using—you have to make sure your contractor uses a vapour barrier liner around any recessed lighting features. This liner—when used properly and Tuck-taped to create a perfect seal—will prevent air movement between the warm zone of your living area and the cold zone above it.

This vapour barrier liner is especially important if you're using spray foam insulation—which is the insulation I recommend for attic ceilings. Batt or blown-in insulation can safely come right up to the sides of the IC box, but spray foam is different. Spray foam expands as it cures—and, since it sprays out as a liquid, it will get into any holes in the IC box. You must have clearance between the foam and the fixture box, which is what the liner provides.

Make sure your contractor talks to your building inspector about the specific requirements in your area for using recessed lights in cold zones.

Get everything on paper

Your final drawing—whether done by you or by a licensed designer or architect—should show the location (including height) of every outlet, light fixture, and appliance. Never assume that your contractor will "just know" what you were hoping for. If it's not on the plan, it's not likely to get done.

Plumbing

Plumbing, like electrical, is an area that you should definitely leave to the pros. It's not likely that anyone would die from plumbing mistakes, but they can be a huge expense to fix, especially when leaks cause damage to drywall, flooring, furniture, etc. Why give yourself that kind of headache? Only work with licensed, experienced plumbers and electricians.

As with so many other aspects of your home, the plumbing you'll find behind your walls depends on the age of the building, since industry standards have changed over the years. You can figure out some things just by looking, if you're willing to take a trip down to your basement or even look under your sinks. But before you can understand what you're seeing, you have to know a little about what you might find.

The plumbing of any house has two basic components: the supply lines (sometimes called the feed lines) and the waste lines or drains. Supply lines carry clean water from the main water intake pipe (usually in your basement) and take it to the various faucets and toilets in your home. All the water may go through a water softener of some kind, and then some of it will split off to the hot water heater. The waste lines take the water and waste from drains and toilets and deposit them into the main stack, which empties into a municipal sewer (or, in a rural area, into your septic system).

Supply lines:
Lead, galvanized, copper—or something new?

For much of the 19th century and the early 20th century, plumbing was made of lead. Over time, it became clear that lead was causing a lot of serious health problems, such as stillbirths and early deaths among babies. Thankfully, most municipalities switched over to galvanized steel for their water supplies as soon as they could, which was a big improvement, but some very old homes might still contain lead plumbing. If you suspect this is the case in your house, you should have it tested and replace it immediately if your suspicions are correct.

Galvanized steel was better than lead, but there were still a lot of problems with it. Because galvanized steel can't repel minerals in the water, scale builds up inside and reduces the amount of water that can pass through. Homeowners see this problem in reduced water pressure, and sometimes in discoloured water coming out of the pipes. The other problem with galvanized steel is that it can corrode and rust, which means that weak spots can suddenly burst. And, in the early years of galvanized steel, some of the zinc applied to the pipes contained lead, which is almost as risky for your health as having lead pipes. Replacing galvanized steel is a good idea.

For supply lines, copper has been the standard material since the 1940s. If your house was built since that time, or has been substantially renovated since that time, chances are you're going to find copper supply lines. That's basically a good thing. Although today there's yet another major change happening in the industry as plumbers move towards flexible plastic piping instead of copper, there's nothing really wrong with copper. It doesn't allow minerals to build up inside the lines, and it's a clean, non-toxic product that's safe for our water. It's relatively flexible and easy to work with, but it does require a lot of time for fitting and soldering joints, which is expensive when you're paying for a highly skilled plumber.

So, if your reno is going to involve new plumbing, what should you do? I'd recommend the new standard of flexible plastic piping, which is a fantastic technology. Because it's flexible, very few junctions are needed. A single manifold in the basement has dedicated feed lines for each faucet, shower, or toilet in the house. You're probably not planning to replace all the plumbing in your house at one time, but you can start with the manifold and just a couple of lines. You can add more lines to the manifold as you renovate other rooms in your house and replace older plumbing lines.

Flexible plastic piping works great with a tankless ("on-demand") hot water system, which I also recommend. There are a lot of cheap versions on the market, but make sure you buy a high-quality, three-stage firing system. You'll be able to run three different hot water sources at the same time (such as a shower, the kitchen sink, and the washing machine). Just remember that you need to run the hot water at a high enough volume for it to work—you have to open the tap, not just let it trickle.

Waste lines: Lead, cast iron, or plastic?

Every water use location in your house—sinks, toilets, showers, and laundry—will have a drain that's connected to a main vent stack. (Larger houses might have a number of vent stacks.) This vent stack is a hollow pipe that should go right through your roof where gases can escape, and at the bottom it empties into the municipal sewer or septic tank.

In older homes it's still common to find vent stacks made of lead or cast iron. We aren't as worried about lead in the waste lines, since the lead is leaching into the waste

MIKE'S TIP

It's all about the installation.

As with almost everything in our homes, the way something is installed matters at least as much as the quality of the materials you're using. So whether you choose copper or flexible plastic piping for your plumbing renovations, keep these installation tips in mind, and speak to your plumber or general contractor if you're concerned:

- Plumbing lines should be run through small holes in the joists and studs, making as little damage to the wooden framing members as possible. Notching into the wood from the side or the bottom is absolutely wrong, and harmful to the structure of the house.

- Copper plumbing should not be run in an exterior wall because the pipes could freeze in the winter.

- To work properly, all plumbing requires air behind water—that is, some air has to be drawn into the system for the water to flow freely. Toilets should always be installed with a proper branch vent to the main stack, not with a "cheater vent" that some people try to get away with. Some building codes allow cheater vents to be used on sinks and bathtubs, but never on toilets. I prefer not to use them at all, but have found myself in situations where the cost difference between installing a cheater vent or doing serious renovation (and repair) work means it made financial sense.

- Ensure that all fixtures are properly installed. The toilet should be solid (it shouldn't rock when you try to move it), and the base should be sealed with silicone caulking.

- A wax ring, not a rubber ring, is the best choice for toilet installation. Wax gives a better seal so there's less chance it will leak.

- Faucets that aren't properly sealed can cause water problems for your counter or cabinets. The faucet should be set into the holes in the counter, and the holes should then be sealed with clear silicone. Once the escutcheon (finishing) plates go on, the plates should be sealed with a bead of clear silicone caulking around the edge.

PVC pipe is the standard for drains that are run underground.

water, not into your drinking water. Still, if you've got walls open for a renovation, now is the time to replace that lead or cast-iron stack with ABS plastic piping. It won't corrode, and won't allow mineral scale to build up either. Replacing a lead or cast-iron stack also means your plumber can avoid the difficulties involved in tying into the old—there are considerable risks of cracks and breaks when working on these old vent stacks.

Beyond the drains inside the house, the main meets up with a line to your street that flows into the municipal sewer. The standard today is to use ABS pipe on all waste lines inside the house, and PVC pipe for any below grade (underground).

As I discussed earlier, older houses might still have an old clay line running from the house to the sewer under your street. If that's the case with your house, I recommend getting a professional inspection done to determine what condition the clay is in, and then replacing the clay with PVC if its time has come.

Take the important step of replacing an outdated drainage system *before* you invest in other renos. You might not enjoy spending the money on something that's invisible, but you sure will regret not doing it if you find your newly finished basement in a foot or more of water and sewage because of a drain backup. Also install a backflow preventer valve to help ensure that this doesn't happen even after improving or updating sanitary lines.

Planning for plumbing

A toilet can be installed anywhere you want, but the cost will be much higher if you want that toilet more than 5 feet away from a vent stack. You'll have the added cost of adding a branch vent, or having to install a new, separate vent stack. That will involve going through floors, ceilings, and the roof to vent it properly, and that will mean flooring, drywall, and roof repairs to any affected rooms.

Be aware too that if you put a toilet in the basement your main sanitary line may be higher than your floor. There are special toilets available that can solve this problem or you can run a new line below the house to the street. This may make sense if there's lots going into the basement like a laundry room and full bath.

If a laundry room is going in the converted attic, make sure there is a drain in the floor to catch water in the event of a washer malfunction.

Design a basement or attic bathroom by thinking about who will be using it, for what purpose, and how often. Will the bathroom be an ensuite for a master bedroom or guest room, a powder room near the family room, a bathroom for a home gym, a practical extra bathroom combined with the laundry room, etc.? This will determine a lot about the design.

Think about how accessible the bathroom should be to living areas, and how to maintain privacy for anyone using the bathroom, especially in terms of the door to the bathroom. Bathroom doors should open into a transitional space, such as a hallway, not directly into a living area.

Consider safety. Leave adequate space around each plumbing fixture, use non-slip flooring, and fit bathtubs and showers with grab bars.

To make sure there's enough space around each fixture, keep the following in mind:

- **For a standard bathtub, allow 60 inches by 32 inches. Allow an "activity area" in front that's at least 44 inches by 28 inches for accessibility.**
- **For a standard washstand (sink set into a vanity, or pedestal sink), you need about 28 inches wide and 24 inches deep. Allow an activity area of at least 40 inches by 28 inches in front of the washstand for clearance.**
- **For a double vanity, allow at least 60 inches in length.**
- **For the toilet and the area in front of it, allow at least 32 inches by 48 inches.**
- **For a bidet, allow the same amount of space as for the toilet, 32 inches by 48 inches.**
- **For a walk-in shower stall, allow at least 32 inches by 32 inches. For more comfort, allow 36 inches. The minimum height for a shower head to be set is 80 inches—but set it higher if people in your house are taller than average. Allow an activity area of 28 inches by 36 inches in front of the shower.**

This is also the time to think about luxury upgrades such as heated towel racks or a bathtub with jets for relaxation.

Plumbing issues in the basement

Basements have unique challenges, and one of them is installing basement bathrooms.

I'm not sure what it is about them, but basement bathroom installations seem to attract contractors who love to work without permits. The fact is that anytime you make changes to your plumbing, you need a permit.

If your contractor says you don't need a permit, stay away from them no matter how good you think they are. If they don't know you need a permit, what else don't they know? If they know and are willing to lie to you, what else are they not telling you the truth about?

The biggest challenge with a basement bathroom can be dealing with the waste plumbing, especially if the main line is underneath the floor—which is usually concrete. Some contractors who do basement bathrooms try to cut corners by installing the drains without breaking up the floor. They'll tell you it's too expensive to break up the concrete, so they suggest you put a raised floor in the bathroom area and then hook up the toilet, sink, and bathtub or shower drain under it to the vertical portion of the existing drain above the floor. It's a bad idea.

A raised floor reduces the ceiling height in an already cramped space, won't provide enough "fall" (downward slope) for the waste pipes, and almost guarantees the rest of the work in the bathroom will be below par.

The problem with breaking up the floor is that it's not fun. It's dusty and dirty, there's heavy concrete to be carried away, and it can be expensive. You need a contractor who insists on breaking up the floor and doing it properly.

If your original basement didn't have a bathroom, there won't be a vent stack your contractor can tie into to vent your toilet, sink, tub, shower, or laundry. It's best to vent the plumbing properly—not with a cheater vent hidden in the wall—and to do that you'll have to run the new vent up to the roof through the house. This will involve drywall and roofing repairs—make no mistake about it.

Basements always contain a lot of moisture, and putting a bathroom down there makes controlling moisture that much more difficult. The cubic feet per minute (CFM) of the bathroom fan should be up around 110 for an average-sized bathroom in the basement, and the vent needs to be directed outside with as few bends as possible. The vent pipe should be 4 inches in diameter.

Basement bathrooms need special care. You're already saving a lot of money by building in your basement rather than having to add onto your house, so don't get stingy by cutting corners.

Plumbing issues in the attic

If basement plumbing is a challenge, attic plumbing is not exactly a walk in the park either. You've got a few problems to overcome.

One, there's the fact that your ceilings are probably sloping, and you may not have a lot of full-height space to use. You can try to focus any fixtures that require full-height ceilings (such as the shower) at the highest point in the room, but quite often that will mean creating a very awkward bathroom. On the positive side, those sloping ceilings will provide you with plenty of low-to-the-floor storage opportunities.

A better solution to height issues is adding a shed dormer (which is a lot wider than a single-window dormer) because it gives you so much usable, full-height space. It can be well worth the expense of adding a dormer if you really want an attic bathroom.

The second problem is waste lines. In the basement, you have to break open the floor and sometimes you have to deal with moving the waste up (defying gravity) to the main drain. In the attic, you have to connect to the main vent stack, which may not be anywhere close to where you want to place your bathroom.

If you can't make the connection, you'll have to install another vent stack, and that means finding a straight run through the floors below, in an inconspicuous place right next to the walls (where it will be enclosed in drywall), and into the basement. But you'll need some luck for everything to line up properly. The only advantage is that you have gravity on your side when it comes to getting rid of the waste.

The third problem is supply lines. As with the waste lines, we need an inconspicuous route for the supply lines to run up to the attic. Ideally, you would be able

MIKE'S TIP

Must-haves in the bathroom

For a renovation that lasts, keep three priorities in mind: quality, safety, and environmental responsibility:

- A good quality exhaust fan that's properly vented outside.
- In faucets, look for ceramic disk or brass ball technology. Avoid plastic or steel for internal fittings.
- In bathtubs, go for heavier and stronger.
- In toilets, look for a wide throat opening at the bottom of the toilet—you want more than the standard 1¾" opening.
- Buy non-slip tile (preferably porcelain) for bathroom floors and shower areas.
- Have grab bars installed in the shower and/or bath area, even if you don't think you need them right now.

to run the supply lines right through the walls. But there's also the question of water pressure. How do we supply water, with adequate flow and pressure, to the highest level of the house? If the water supply line coming in from your house is correct, then this shouldn't be a problem.

Finally, there's the issue of getting large plumbing fixtures into your attic in the first place. The time to do this is while you're still at the framing stage, when you don't have to manoeuvre around finished walls. Before purchasing any fixture for your attic bathroom, discuss this issue with your general contractor and/or plumber, and make sure you measure everything.

HVAC (heating, ventilation, and air conditioning)

The heat source in a house is part of what's called the mechanical system. Mechanicals include everything that can be grouped under HVAC systems—heating, ventilation, and air conditioning. So the person who installs and fixes your heating system might be known as a heating contractor, a mechanical contractor, or an HVAC contractor.

Placing your furnace and water heater in a mechanical room is a good idea. Just make sure that there's adequate air flow for them to function properly.

Whenever you expand your house in some way, your heating contractor will need to be consulted about how that extra space will be heated and cooled without upsetting the balance of your current heating system. Even though both the basement and attic have always been part of the building envelope, they probably haven't been heated spaces. When you convert either or both into living space, you're actually expanding your house, and your heating and cooling load may need to be addressed.

Let's look at why this is a concern.

Normally, when a home is built, the furnace that's installed is sized to heat and cool a space that's about 10% more than the actual size of your home. If you add substantially to your square footage—whether you finish your basement or attic, or actually build on with an addition—you may need to replace your furnace, and possibly your central air conditioning unit.

Again, normally, your furnace will be able to handle the extra load of a basement or attic, but not always.

But it's important to know this: bigger is not necessarily better. That's because when it comes to efficient heating, having a furnace that's the right size—not the biggest—is even more important than having a top-of-the-line, high-efficiency furnace.

"Right-sizing" your furnace

You hear a lot about a furnace being so-many-percent efficient. That percentage number is actually the annual fuel utilization efficiency (AFUE). It measures the percentage of energy converted into usable heat. The higher the percentage, the more efficient the furnace.

If your furnace is ten years old or more, it's probably in the 60% to 70% AFUE range. In other words, you're wasting thirty to forty cents on every dollar you spend for heat. Newer furnaces are more in the 80% area for medium efficiency, and 90% for high efficiency.

The efficiency of the furnace and the size of your house determine how big your furnace should be. Furnace sizes are measured in heating capacity—BTUs (British thermal units), the standard measure for heat transfer capacity. When the size of your house changes, your furnace may need to change too.

As you plan your basement or attic conversion, consult your heating contractor about your furnace's capacity. They'll take a look at the size of your house—including the areas that you plan to turn into living space—and various components of your house's "shell" to determine the proper furnace size. They'll take into account the square footage, the amount of insulation, the siding, the type and number of windows, doors, shingles, and so on. This gives your heating contractor an idea of how many BTUs it will take to keep your house continuously heated. This number is your home's new "heat load."

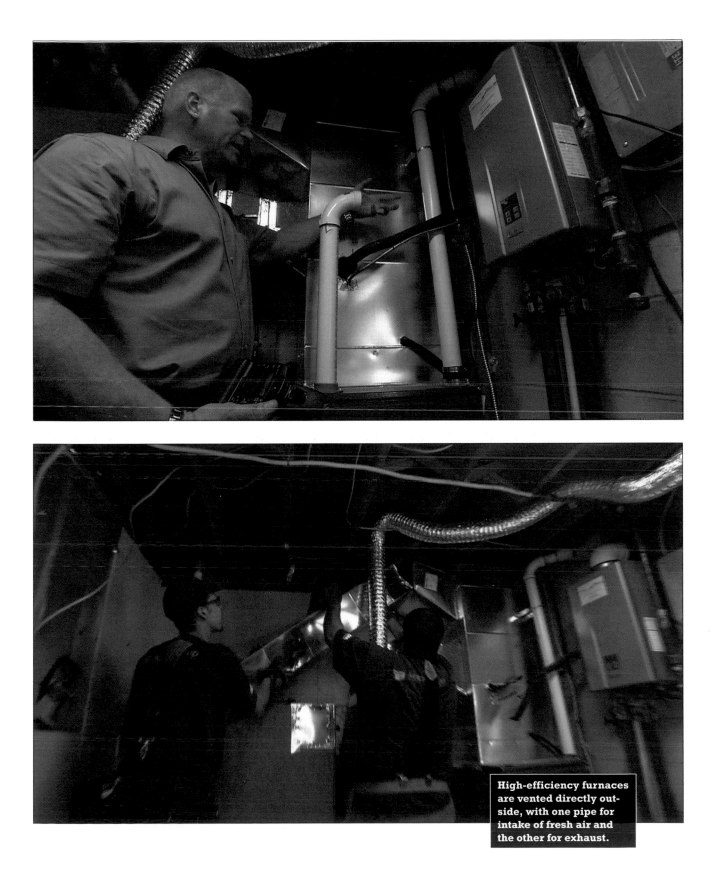

High-efficiency furnaces are vented directly outside, with one pipe for intake of fresh air and the other for exhaust.

Let's say that your heating contractor takes a look at your plans for an expanded house and calculates the new heat load at 61,500 BTU. An 80,000 BTU furnace that's 80% efficient provides 64,000 BTU, so it's a good fit. So would it be better to have an 80,000 BTU furnace that's 90% efficient?

No! Here's why: The higher efficiency furnace produces 72,000 BTU—too much for the house. That means your home will never reach proper comfort levels because the heat will rise faster than it takes to cycle the cold air through the furnace. That's called "short cycling," and it's bad.

Putting in too much furnace is a practice known as "oversizing." It leads to short firing cycles, which means the furnace never gets to burn fuel at peak capacity. It also means the furnace never gets hot enough to dry out, so condensation forms, which then leads to corrosion of the furnace. It's like driving a car on short trips. The exhaust system stays wet and rusts out prematurely.

Not only does the furnace wear out, its fuel efficiency drops.

Also, remember we're dealing with two kinds of efficiency here. So far, we've been talking about the fuel used to heat the house, not the fuel (electricity) to run the fan. It doesn't matter what the efficiency of the furnace is, electrical consumption on the fan is going to be about the same no matter what. In fact, some newer furnaces use bigger blowers and draft fans that actually use more electricity.

Bottom line: one size does not fit all. Get the right size furnace for your newly expanded house by consulting a qualified and experienced heating contractor who will calculate your house's new heat load.

There are other options, however. You might be able to use a supplementary form of heat to make up the extra heat load. Radiant in-floor heat, fireplaces, and electric heat are just a few of the options I'll outline in the next few pages.

About radiant in-floor heat

Radiant heat is both the newest and oldest type of heating there is. Advanced forms of radiant heat date back hundreds of years.

The kind of radiant heat you might be most familiar with is the old (but still very efficient) system of boiler and radiators. Many homes today still have cast-iron radiators filled with water. Those radiators are connected to a boiler unit in the basement that heats the water that runs through the whole system. If you've got this kind of radiant heat in your house, I strongly recommend that you keep it.

Radiant heat—whether from radiators or in-floor heating systems—is comfortable and efficient and it doesn't send dust and allergens through the air the way a forced air system does. The downside of a boiler system is that your room temperature can't be adjusted as quickly as it could be with a forced air furnace.

There are many types of in-floor radiant heat products on the market. The hydronic systems are water-based. What's installed is a type of plastic piping that loops horizontally across the floor, with the loops set 6 inches, 9 inches, or 12 inches apart. The pipes contain water or glycol that's heated from a central manifold, usually located in the basement of your house.

Another type of in-floor heat is electric. Very small wires are looped into a thin mat that's installed under your flooring. You can buy it in ready-made mats in various sizes, or have the mats customized. The mats can't be customized on-site, so using this product requires careful planning ahead of time. It shouldn't be used under hardwood flooring, but is perfect under ceramic or stone flooring.

In-floor heating can be excellent for small spaces such as bathrooms, kitchens, or even additions. And since the heat can be adjusted on a zone-by-zone basis, you have a lot of control.

One drawback to in-floor heating systems is the possibility of damage to the system if a nail or screw is ever driven through the floor and into the piping or electric mat. It can be repaired, but the repair can be costly.

Fireplaces as supplementary heat

A fireplace is an asset to almost any room. Everybody loves being near a fireplace, which means that you'll enjoy using it and you'll find it a valuable selling feature if you ever want to sell your house.

With the addition of a fireplace, though, you could find that the rest of your house isn't as warm as it should be. The problem might be the location of your thermostat.

If you install a gas fireplace in your living room—which is where the thermostat is usually located—you could end up with a situation where your fireplace is competing with the furnace. The fireplace will warm up the living room, causing the thermostat to read a higher temperature than in the rest of the house. The thermostat will "think" that the whole house is warmer than it really is, and won't send a signal to the furnace to start up.

The solution is to relocate your thermostat to another interior wall, farther from the fireplace. This should get your furnace to function properly again, and make the whole house more comfortable.

A traditional wood fireplace doesn't provide the most energy efficient type of heating, since most of the heat created by the flames goes right up the chimney. The open combustion draws air from your home to keep the fire going. This is the warm air you'd rather have staying in your home. Older masonry fireplaces have efficiency ratings of less than 10%, which means that most of your heating money is wasted. And of course, when the fire isn't lit, there's often a noticeable draft coming down the chimney.

Older wood-burning masonry fireplaces are often drafty and inefficient, so many homeowners decide to install an insert. This is basically a sealed wood stove that gets placed into the open fireplace. Wood stoves and inserts are made of steel or cast

Traditional wood-burning fireplaces are not the most energy efficient type of heating, but inserts and newer fireplaces with blowers can be a great option.

iron and they have glass doors so you can see the flames inside. There are blowers and fans that distribute heat into the room.

Wood stoves and inserts still require proper venting and need to be connected safely to your chimney, with a stainless steel chimney liner. Inserts can also be used to change a wood-burning fireplace into one that burns gas or wood pellets.

A wood stove or insert is much more efficient than a traditional wood fireplace— offering between 70% and 80% efficiency. It's a closed-door system that allows for complete combustion, which greatly reduces emissions.

So can you rely on this type of heat in a basement or attic? It's possible, but not ideal.

The first challenge is exhaust. Consult a qualified heating specialist to find out if it's feasible to install a wood stove or insert in the place you have in mind, and check with your municipality to find out about its installation laws. Unlike gas fireplaces, which can be directly vented to the outside through a wall, venting a wood stove can require expensive retrofitting of an existing chimney, or the construction of a new chimney, and you may be better off putting your dollars elsewhere. If you have the freedom to run the stovepipe inside and directly through the roof, you may have lower costs. Keep in mind too that it's possible the fireplace will pull too much air from the house to feed the fire because it doesn't have its own air supply or the house doesn't have an HRV unit. This can lead to negative air pressure, which is both serious and dangerous.

Second, consider that any heat source that uses wood as fuel will require work on your part—all the time. You can't set a thermostat and make sure the temperature stays in a comfortable range. You can't set it at a low temperature to keep the pipes

from freezing when you go away for a few days. If you're going to have plumbing in the room, you'll need a backup source of heat, such as in-floor heat or even some sort of electric heater.

Another challenge with a wood stove is that good firewood can be expensive and hard to find in adequate quantities for heating, and you'll need to haul, stack, and move the wood before it ever reaches the fireplace. You'll also need a substantial amount of space (covered and dry, though not inside your home) to store it, if you're planning to use wood for heating rather than just atmosphere from time to time. Only seasoned firewood (meaning that it's been stored in a shed or under a tarp to keep it dry for about a year) can be used for fuel, since wet or green wood smokes and won't burn properly.

An alternative to burning wood is to use fuel pellets in a wood pellet furnace. Leftover sawdust from the lumber industry is compressed under high pressure into pellets, with no added glue for binding. The pellets can also be made from wood chips, bark, recycled paper, shelled corn, wheat, and sunflower seeds. Another option is fast-growing switchgrass—a great renewable energy crop since switchgrass grows quickly on marginal land and is usually considered a "waste" product.

You don't need to regularly feed the fire like in a wood-burning stove since the pellets can be fed into the fire from a storage hopper and furnaces are self-igniting. And unlike a wood-burning stove, you can control the heat with a thermostat. You do need electricity to run a wood-pellet stove since the hot air is blown through a heat exchanger, so that's a drawback, especially if you might be looking for a type of backup heat in the case of power outages.

Gas fireplaces are easy to use, there's no wood to chop, you just flip a switch. Many homeowners may think that the "fires" look fake, but newer fireplaces have more realistic flames. Gas doesn't spark like a wood fireplace, so there's no chance of sparks damaging your floors or furniture.

I recommend that you get an electricity-free ignition so that if your power goes out, you still have a heat source, although many gas fireplaces are dependent on electricity to run the blower fan too.

Natural gas burns cleaner than wood, but if your gas fireplace isn't adjusted properly, it can create a lot of pollution through incomplete combustion—and can also produce carbon monoxide, which is deadly in high enough concentrations. You should have a hard-wired carbon monoxide detector to protect you from this.

There's more flexibility with placing and installing a gas fireplace than a wood-burning one. They can use an existing chimney, and you can also get direct-vent models that exhaust straight through an exterior wall.

Gas fireplaces are becoming more efficient all the time. With sealed combustion, direct-vent fireplaces reportedly work at 90% efficiency. With such high efficiency, they can be a viable option for heating an attic or basement space.

Electric fireplaces are less costly to buy and install than gas or masonry, but they aren't cheap to run, since the cost of electricity doesn't seem to be going down. Electric fireplaces have artificial logs and a light fixture that looks like a real fireplace. They're basically light bulbs, or LED light fixtures, behind a screen that looks like flame. Since there's no flame and no fumes, they don't need a vent or a chimney.

Some electric fireplaces have a heating element and a fan to circulate the warmth into the room. Most have different switches and settings that allow you to operate them with just flame, or with heat and flame, and at different temperature settings, controlled by an adjustable thermostat. They may not provide as much heat as a gas or masonry fireplace, and your electric fireplace is on its own circuit. Often people will overload their electrical circuits by using the electric fireplace on a circuit that's serving other loads. This could trip your breakers or even start a fire. If you're planning to use an electric fireplace that plugs in, talk to your electrician.

Alcohol or gel fuel fireplaces use denatured ethanol—which is an alcohol that comes from fermented sugar cane, corn, potatoes, beets, or cereal grain.

Ethanol burns clear and is odour and smoke free, so it's safe to burn indoors. The byproducts of combustion are simply carbon dioxide and water vapour. Gelled alcohol is safe to store inside at room temperature.

Alcohol fireplaces are completely free standing and don't need a chimney or venting, so you can place them anywhere in a room. If you live in a very airtight house, it could be a concern that not enough air will be available to run the fireplace properly; you need to make sure there's air to draw from. But in most houses there will be an adequate supply of air through normal infiltration and venting.

Alcohol fireplaces will add heat to your room like any fireplace, but they are not really intended to be used as a regular heat source.

Heating and cooling issues in the basement

If your basement was completely unfinished prior to starting your reno, you may have only one or two air vents bringing in conditioned air—or sometimes none at all.

There might be one or two cold-air returns, but probably your biggest air return is the staircase that leads to your main floor.

To determine how much more heat you'll need in the basement, and how the ductwork will need to be adjusted, consult your heating contractor.

You may be able to heat the basement just by adding a couple of openings in the ductwork. Consider a gas fireplace and/or radiant in-floor heat if you're looking for more comfort or ambiance.

No matter what else you do in terms of additional heat sources, remember that your basement will only be as comfortable as the insulation you've installed. Make sure walls and floors are insulated with a proper thermal break. During the hot months of the year, you'll find that insulation will also help to keep the basement cool and dry rather than humid.

Heating and cooling issues in the attic

I'm sure it won't come as a surprise to you when I say that heating an attic is easier than cooling it. That's because hot air is pushed by cold, which is a real bonus in the winter: your attic will get some of the warm air that's pushed upwards through your house.

In the summer, that hot air is another matter. Hot air continues to rise to the upper level of your house, and it can be tough to get enough cool air to the attic on

A good HVAC contractor can help address the challenges of keeping an attic warm in the winter and cool in the summer.

MIKE'S TIP

A common problem

The number one complaint I hear from homeowners is how cold the room is above their garages. Often the ceiling in the garage is not properly insulated, which allows cold or warm air, and even exhaust fumes, to escape into the room. Good insulation, such as a closed-cell polyurethane spray foam, which stops air movement, can make a huge difference.

the hottest days of the year. With a typical forced air furnace and ductwork, you may find that the cool air from your air conditioner is a lot less cool and refreshing than you'd like by the time it arrives at your attic level.

There are two issues here. The first is simply that the air has to travel a long way: from the furnace and air conditioning unit in your basement, up at least two and maybe three levels. The blower has to be strong enough to push that cold air upwards—and remember that cool air has a tendency to fall. The second issue is that unsealed ductwork can allow the cool air to leak out along the way.

The solution to these problems is fairly simple. Discuss this with your heating contractor, who should determine whether the blower can handle the extra distance that the cool air has to travel. They should also ensure that any accessible ductwork has been properly sealed and insulated to prevent air leaks.

Remember that there are two types of ducts in a forced air system: supply and return. Supply ducts bring conditioned (heated or cooled) air into your rooms. The return ducts (the big vents at the bottom or top of your walls, or on the floor) draw air from each room to be sent back to the heating/cooling system.

It's like a loop. The air goes into your room and has to return to the heating source to finish the loop. Air won't move unless it's forced to. Forced air systems create a pressure difference and will push and pull air throughout your house.

Most North American forced air systems still use sheet metal ducts, which are joined and seamed together when assembled. But these seams can leak and the joints might come loose.

Most of the ducts you see inside your house are leaky and aren't insulated. That's not necessarily a problem because you're leaking warm (or cool) air into other rooms that you want warm (or cool) anyway, but it does prevent the heat from getting to its proper destination, which may be why some rooms are colder (or warmer) than they should be. This can be especially challenging if you're trying to force air into an upper-level room, such as an attic.

If the system is very leaky, you'll not only have problems getting the air to a comfortable temperature throughout your house, you'll also be wasting your money. Leaks in a forced air duct system are a major source of energy waste—up to 25%! This happens when hot or cool air leaks out in places where you don't need it. For example, ductwork may run through a garage, unfinished basement, or crawlspace, and a leak in a supply duct means heated or cooled air might be pouring into these areas.

Make sure your reno plans include an assessment of your ductwork, and that any exposed ductwork—especially in unheated areas—is well sealed with foil tape (not duct tape) and insulated. You'll see a big difference in your home's comfort level and also in your fuel bills.

One final note on making your attic cool in summer: insulating the ceiling and walls properly will pay off in a big way. Use closed-cell polyurethane foam insulation, sprayed onto the underside of the roof, followed by a layer of rigid foam insulation to cover any thermal "bridges," such as rafters. You'll find that your house is more "immune" to the temperature outside—whether hot or cold—because of the complete thermal break you'll get from those layers of high-performing insulation. Other forms of insulation just can't compare.

Following up: Checklist for electrical

❏ Does your contractor work only with licensed electricians? Ask about this, and be sure that only a licensed electrician is allowed to work in your home.

❏ Do you have electrical issues throughout the house? If so, set your priorities as follows. First, address safety issues. Second, upgrade the panel to the level you need. Third, run new wiring for areas being renovated. Fourth, upgrade other electrical as needed.

❏ Have you thought about where you want overhead lighting, floor lamps, task lighting, etc.? Plan every aspect of your lighting and other electrical needs, and ensure these are written into the final design drawing for both your contractor and electrician to see.

Following up: Checklist for plumbing

❏ Have you checked with your general contractor about their plumber's qualifications? Hire only licensed plumbers to do the work.

❏ Does your house have an old drainage system that should be replaced? While you're working on the basement is the most sensible time to think of replacing it. This includes replacing the old cast-iron or lead vent stack with black ABS piping, and replacing the waste lines under the floor and out to the municipal sewer lines with white PVC pipes.

❏ Are backflow preventers legal in your municipality, and does your home have one? If possible, install a backflow preventer as insurance against backups and flooding.

❏ Do your basement or attic plans involve a new bathroom, laundry room, etc.? If so, consider using a system of flexible plastic piping for any new plumbing.

Following up:
Checklist for HVAC

❏ **Will your reno plans affect your heat load? Consult an HVAC specialist to do a heat loss calculation of your house.**

❏ **Is it time for a new furnace? If so, install a new, "right-sized," high-efficiency furnace.**

❏ **How are you planning to heat that newly finished basement or attic? A new furnace may be enough, or you may choose to supply the extra heat you need with radiant in-floor heat, a high-efficiency fireplace, or a form of electric heat.**

❏ **Is your insulation good enough to keep heating and cooling costs down? For maximum efficiency and comfort, ensure the area is insulated with a proper thermal break.**

CHAPTER 4

Hiring Right and Working with Your Contractor

A good general contractor is the key to a successful renovation. There's no two ways about it: the general contractor you hire has the power to make or break the outcome of your reno. It's worth every bit of time and effort it takes to find the right person because it will affect your home, your pocketbook, and even your health.

A bad general contractor, on the other hand, costs you money—sometimes, a lot of it. They could leave you with a reno that's so badly done your house is actually worth *less* than before the work started. I've heard and seen too many examples of how a bad contractor has almost cost people their home and their marriage. A bad general contractor can cause damage to your property, not to mention the damage that's harder to see: the time you'll spend dealing with the problems; the disruption to your life; and the frustration, anger, and disappointment. You were looking forward to great results, not pain and suffering.

In the following pages, I'm going to tell you how to find a good general contractor, how to put together a contract that protects you, and how to be the kind of client who gets great results.

First, let's be clear about what I mean when I say "general contractor."

A general contractor will either do or contract out all the work on your job. They will find out what you want; come up with a plan, budget, and timeline for getting it done; and oversee the whole project from start to finish. The general contractor will find and hire anyone needed for the job, from designers and engineers to carpenters, drywallers, electricians, plumbers, etc. The general contractor will also do all the scheduling so that the subcontractors (tradespeople) complete their part of the job on time, smoothly paving the way for the next trade. The general contractor is your go-to person, the one who deals with any problems or questions along the way.

There are other kinds of contractors too. Specialty contractors make their living doing specific jobs, such as kitchen or bathroom renovations. For electrical, plumbing, and heating and cooling work, you need a trade contractor. You should always go with someone who is licensed. In every province and territory in Canada, there are different licensing requirements for people who work in the trades. Your provincial government's website should be able to direct you to information on licensing in your region.

What you really need to ask

Here are some general questions to ask any contractor you're thinking of hiring, no matter what the job. Remember, I always say that finding a good contractor can take as long—or longer—than doing the job itself.

How long have you been in business?

A longer time (measured in years, not months) usually indicates that the general contractor is experienced, and good enough to stay in business. And how long have they and their company been around? If they've been in business for twenty-five years but their company has only been incorporated for one year, that's a bad sign. What did they do previously? Did they change company names to avoid being sued?

Are you licensed and insured? Do you make sure all your employees and subcontractors are also insured, and licensed whenever a licence is required? Can you provide proof of insurance and licensing in writing?

This is critical, and the proof of licensing and insurance is something that will become part of any contract you sign.

Can you give me some names of past customers that I can call for references?

Ask for at least five or six references—the more, the better; don't be shy. This is your house and your money. Your job now is to contact (or, when possible, visit) the references. You'd be surprised how many people make the mistake of not doing this. If a contractor is unable or unwilling to provide you with references, cross them off your list. Once you make contact with the references, ask lots of questions. Was the contractor on time, were they professional, did they call you back quickly, did they leave the site clean every day, was there a good team of tradespeople on the job? Have you had any problems with your reno? Did it cost more than budgeted? Why?

Do you have any ideas or suggestions about this project?
If the contractor's a pro, they'll probably be thinking of ways to make your project work better or give you better value for your money.

Can I get a ballpark figure?
The contractor won't be able to give you a hard-and-fast estimate at first glance, but they should be able to give you a general idea. Just keep in mind that this needs to be done carefully. Avoid price comparisons if you can see that the work being offered (including materials and skill set) isn't comparable from one contractor to the next.

When could you start and how long do you think it would take?
Most contractors worth the money aren't available at a moment's notice. Be suspicious if they say they can start tomorrow.

Getting quotes

Once you've interviewed and checked references, you'll have a short list. Time to get down to dollars and cents. The trick here is to make sure everyone is bidding on the same thing. It's your responsibility to make sure the information is the same for every contractor. If you don't provide adequate plans and specifications, each contractor will decide how they'll carry out the work and what materials they'll use. That's going to give you an "apples and oranges" situation, and that's no good for anybody.

First, you need plans and specifications so that each contractor can quote on the same thing. Plans include the drawings, diagrams, or sketches that describe the work to be done. These drawings will also be required to obtain a building permit. You could hire a registered designer, architect, or even a general contractor to draw up plans (which would mean paying for this service), or you could use your own diagrams (either computer generated or hand drawn—whatever you're most comfortable with). If you pay a contractor for this service, you shouldn't feel obligated to have them do the actual work. Specifications are the details—a list of products and materials to be used in the project that can include brand names, model numbers, and even colours.

What you see.
What I see.

You see well-placed pot lights in the basement. If insulation for sound-proofing has been put in the ceiling, I'd want to make sure that pot lights that can come in contact with insulation have been used.

A beautiful wall unit for a home entertainment system. It's important in any reno to plan ahead. When the walls are down, think about putting in plastic pipes for wire runs so you can easily run new wiring if you need to make changes in the future.

Good to see a smoke detector here. I'd like to make sure that it's hardwired and interconnected with all the detectors in the house so if there's a fire in the basement all the detectors go off.

You see a fully finished ceiling. I'd want to know what's behind these bulkheads. If it's heating vents, how has the drywall been attached? I've seen houses where the drywall is installed so sloppily that there are screw holes in the heating vents and heat is leaking out.

You see a basement window that gives great natural light. I see potential mould and water damage if the window and window well have not been installed properly.

Now use the plans and specifications to get contractor bids.

As you compare bids, look for value and quality, not just price. Think about what each contractor will bring to the job, especially in terms of the workmanship you saw or heard about when you checked out their references. And keep in mind that the contractor with the lowest price might not understand the job, or may be underestimating the time it will take.

Finally, go with your gut. Ask yourself how you feel about each contractor. Do you feel confident about them? Will you be able to communicate with them comfortably? You're going to be working with this person for a while, so personality matters. But don't fall for the smoothest talker. Pay attention to what the contractor's actually saying.

Detailed drawings and specifications allow contractors to make bids you can really compare.

MIKE'S TIP

What is the right price?

Three seems to be the magic number for many homeowners when looking for contractors and getting quotes. Then what? When you have a high, medium, and low quote, many people figure the right choice is the middle price. The right price has nothing to do with the highest, lowest, or medium price. It has everything to do with using the right products in your home, installed the right way. Use plans and detailed specifications when you get quotes and compare apples to apples. All the materials, including the stuff you don't see, like a subfloor, should be in your quote to help determine the right price. You may only need to talk to three contractors and look at three quotes, but you're likely going to talk to many more contractors if you want the right one at the right price.

Now get it in writing!

I know what you're thinking: more details on paper before the work can even begin. It can feel like this part of the process takes forever. But a contract is your blueprint for how and when the work is expected to be done, and what it will cost, including how to deal with unforeseen delays or costs. Taking the time to get this part right will help you avoid sticky situations (or even legal messes) in the future.

At its most basic, the contract needs to cover two types of information:

1. Every aspect of the project you and the contractor have agreed to, including work to be done, material and product specifications, responsibility for building permits and inspections, the work schedule, price and payment arrangements, and the process for making change orders (you'll see more on change orders in the next section). The payment schedule should always be built around project benchmarks, not arbitrary dates on the calendar. Remember that at the end of the day the homeowner is always on the hook—legally—for getting the permits, even if you've decided the contractor will get them for you.

2. Proof that the contractor is operating their business properly, so you're protected from risks. This includes proof of business liability insurance, Workers' Compensation coverage or equivalent accidental injury insurance, proof of bonding and/or licensing where the government requires it, and proof of proper business registration (a business or GST/HST number).

Managing "extras"

If you stop and put your imagination to work on other things that might come up on the job, you can probably predict a few other items that need to be in your contract.

The first is a hot-button topic for contractors and homeowners alike: "extras." These are things that are added to the original agreement and that can end up taking a lot more time, and costing more, than you planned.

Most pros have a pretty good idea of what's behind the walls just because of the age of the building, but they may not be able to predict the condition of what they'll find,

Upgrading to a tankless water heater when renovating is a good bet since they save energy and are more compact than traditional tank-style water heaters.

or how much will be required to fix or work around it. When the walls of your house are opened up during the reno, your contractor will sometimes find things they weren't expecting—old knob-and-tube wiring, for example, in a house that's already had substantial work done on it in recent years, including supposedly "updated" electrical.

So how do you manage extras with your contractor? Your guiding principle should be fairness. What's fair? Whose choice—or mistake—caused the extra? Did you change your mind about something after the contract was signed and the bid accepted? Should the contractor—the professional and the expert in this relationship—have predicted the extra and included it into the fixed price?

Here's an example that happened on one of my projects: we pulled up the floor tile of a bad kitchen renovation and discovered a bare wire buried in the mortar. We looked further and discovered hidden junction boxes, hot wires dead-ended in walls, and dozens of other code violations waiting to burn down the house.

There was no way we could have anticipated wiring so bad, and no way we could leave it as it was. If your contractor finds a situation like that, it's fair to charge an extra to the contract to fix it. Of course, they'll have to explain it to you and have you sign off on the extra work and cost—before they start to work, not after.

Before the work starts, a good contractor will have given you a list detailing the decisions you have to make to keep the project on time and on budget. Bathroom fixtures, cabinets, stairs, doors, and windows all have lead times, and if you don't get your first choice in time to meet the work schedule, there's a chance you could be charged for delays or corrections to accommodate you. Delays cost money as well as time, and sometimes you need to pay a premium to rush orders so you can avoid further delays.

Your contractor can't read your mind, so if you make changes that are clearly not part of the original contract, you should expect to pay for them. If you change your mind on the colour of the paint, or the flooring, or the built-ins, what's fair then hinges on the cost of materials and how those changes affect the work schedule. Changes to the work schedule cost your contractor extra time and money—beyond the initial contract price.

There are two ways that these extra costs can be handled.

One way is to set aside a contingency budget in the contract. A contingency budget allows you and the contractor to resolve specific details as the work progresses. If unexpected costs arise, you'll have the funds to amend the contract accordingly.

Another way is to allow for change orders along the way, as needed. A change order is an amendment to your contract. When a hidden deficiency is discovered, or you, the homeowner, change your mind about something and deviate from the original work plan, the contractor will write up a summary of the costs involved and the extra time it will take. Once you've approved the summary, and you've both signed it, it becomes part of the contract—in fact, it's as legally binding as the contract itself.

Unscrupulous contractors will enter a low initial bid and then pounce on extras as a way of increasing their margins. If you get a price that is substantially lower than the others and you go for it, watch out for pricey extras. And by the same token, don't think you can hire a contractor for a fixed price, and then expect them to "throw it in" every time you change your mind or there's an unpredicted (and unpredictable) surprise.

Good planning from the beginning will reduce the number of extras you'll have, and the best way to control your costs is to keep extras down. A good contractor will handle extras properly by including a fair pricing procedure for them in the original contract. They'll charge in one of two ways—time and material, or fixed price.

Roofing is one area where bad contractors often take shortcuts, such as not stripping back all layers of shingles or taking the time to install a ridge vent properly. Here the proper processes are depicted.

MIKE'S TIP

Permits and inspections

If your contractor will be getting permits for your project, your job isn't done. Building permits tell us what we can build; it is the building inspector's job to make sure the contractor did what the permit allowed, and did it properly. A lot of homeowners worry about visits by the building inspector, but inspectors can be your allies.

The inspector (or inspectors) will likely be in more than once, to do their inspection in stages. How many times exactly the inspector goes through depends on the complexity of the job. Don't worry: your permit will outline exactly when you need inspections, as well as who you must call to set them up. And once you've made that first contact with the inspectors, they will always tell you when another inspection is required.

Both you and your contractor should be there whenever an inspector comes to call—if there are four different building inspectors, make sure that you are there for the four different appointments. You both need to know if there are any problems to be rectified, and your contractor needs to know that *you* know. This keeps them from telling you that everything was fine even when it wasn't. Do not trust the word of anyone but the inspector. How many times have I heard some homeowner with a disaster on their hands say, "Oh, they said everything had passed," only to find out the inspector had never been there at all. Do not—repeat, *do not*— go any further at each stage, or allow your contractor to go any further, without confirming it with your building inspector. An inspection's primary purpose is to ensure that minimum code is being met by your contractor, but it's useful for other reasons, too. As the homeowner, you are assured that the job is being done right.

Whenever possible, go with a fixed-price approach. And make sure that extras cannot proceed without a written and signed change order from you. Pros know how long something (without changes or surprises) is likely to take.

Contracts are worth the hassle

No one likes the process of coming up with a thorough, detailed contract. But let me be crystal clear about this: avoid the temptation to bypass this important step. The two things you really should not do are "seal the deal" with a handshake only, or worse, "go underground" by agreeing to a cash-only arrangement.

The first situation is obviously a bad idea: if a disagreement arises, you've got nothing in writing to support your position.

The second situation is even worse. It's risky because the cash market doesn't protect you from risks related to poor work or dishonesty by the contractor, and it could leave you liable for thousands (or even millions) if someone gets injured on the job.

You might also think that by hiring a contractor for cash, you don't have anything to worry about. After all, it's the contractor who's breaking the law, right? Well, yes and no. If a contractor isn't reporting income and paying taxes, they won't want their name turning up on other government records like Workers' Compensation files, business license applications, or building permits.

So where would that leave you?

For one thing, it would leave you without a building permit—which you need for almost any residential renovation. It's the property owner, not the contractor, who is legally responsible for meeting building code and permit requirements. If a permit is required, and a municipal building inspector finds out you didn't get one, they can put a stop to the work until a permit is in place, or even order the work torn down at your expense.

That's just one example. There are a number of other laws that can affect you if you hire underground—things like Workers' Compensation, consumer protection against overcharging, security of deposits, and construction liens. New-home warranty programs won't apply if you're having a renovation done. Without a legal, above-board working relationship with your contractor, where will you turn if something goes wrong?

Construction work involves risks. When someone works on your home, you need to be protected. Just because the job is simple or small doesn't mean something can't go wrong.

When it comes to contracts, there are just a few basic principles to follow: Work with pros. Stay legitimate. And put everything in writing.

As I've said again and again, hiring right is probably the most important decision you'll make during a renovation. Get the right person for the job, and put together a contract that spells out everything you can think of. Remember that the point of the contract isn't to create some weapon you can use in court. The point of the contract is to ensure everyone is clear on what the project is, what the schedule is, and how to get the job done successfully.

Once the contract is in place, always make sure that you're fulfilling your part of the agreement, especially in terms of payments and scheduling. Be fair and reasonable, and you might be surprised at how much more you'll enjoy the process.

A contract checklist

Before you sign the contract:

- ❏ **Check the contractor's references.**
- ❏ **Know exactly what you want.**
- ❏ **Iron out every detail of cost, scheduling, and design, as well as managing extras.**
- ❏ **Have a realistic budget, and set a payment schedule in the written contract.**
- ❏ **Do your homework so you understand the job almost as well as the contractor does.**

Once the work has begun:

- ❏ **Start a job log.**
- ❏ **Conduct regular meetings.**
- ❏ **Bring up concerns immediately and respectfully to your contractor only and not the trades (electricians, plumbers, etc.).**
- ❏ **Take photos before, during, and after.**
- ❏ **Never relax your expectations.**
- ❏ **Fulfill your part of the agreement.**
- ❏ **If you must make changes, detail them in a change order.**

Workplace safety: How you can help

Not too long ago, one of my crew members lost a family member in a workplace accident. It was a terrible tragedy that this young man lost his life, and that loss will affect his family, friends, and co-workers forever. For me it was a reminder that all of us need to work safely, and that you as a homeowner also need to make sure your contractor is working safely.

It's shocking to me that on average five workers die in Canada every workday on job sites, and many more are injured in falls or workplace accidents. Every work site has potential hazards: chemicals, heavy equipment, and power tools, for example.

Workers can get heat stroke from high temperatures or frostbite from the cold. They can slip, trip, or fall from a height.

I'm not saying that you, as the homeowner, have to be on-site as the safety officer, but you should be aware of the basics. And those basics start when you hire your contractor. Ask the right questions and you can play a role in reducing injuries on the job.

Ask your contractor about their health and safety record. Ask for proof of Workers' Compensation coverage. Ask if they have any safety training, and what their health and safety practices are. Ask if the contractor will make sure the workers wear and use personal protective equipment (PPE). That means hard hats and CSA-approved safety boots, eye and ear protection, work gloves, fall-arrest gear if they're working at a height above 3 metres, dust masks, and respirators.

Check that the contractor will have a properly stocked first-aid kit on-site at all times. That kit should include bandages, ointments, dressings, gauze, cold compresses, burn treatments, emergency eye care, and pain-relief products.

Once your contractor has begun the job, make sure they're keeping safety in mind. Is the job site clean? My biggest pet peeve is a dirty job site—if the floors are slippery from sawdust, and construction debris is scattered around, it's a recipe for disaster. I've told the story of when I was working with my dad and how he kept on telling me to clean up, and I said I'd get around to it. I put up a ladder over a hole in the floor that was covered in debris—down I went. Nothing was hurt but my dignity. But it could have been much worse.

Clean-up is a big part of the job. Garbage and scrap has to be constantly picked up and put into bins and dumpsters and kept away from walkways, stairs, and other traffic paths. Or, if there's no bin, make sure the contractor is piling garbage and scrap into a single, out-of-the-way spot.

MIKE'S TIP

Let your insurance company know.
Before your contractor starts work, talk to them and to your insurance company. Your contractor should have liability insurance and Workers' Compensation to cover damages or injuries. Ask to see a current insurance certificate to be sure. For your own liability, normal coverage may be fine, but you need to make sure that you're covered for the scope of your renovation. It's worth a call.

A clean job site is a sign of a good contractor. Messy sites can be unsafe and can be a red flag that you've hired the wrong contractor.

If the workers are on your roof or on the edge of an upper floor, they should be protected by a sturdy guardrail or be wearing proper fall-arrest equipment—a safety belt or harness—that's been properly secured.

Is your contractor excavating around your foundation? Is the trench properly sloped back to prevent collapse or cave-in? Or is it properly supported by a shoring system?

Are there young workers or apprentices on the job? If so, that's great—I respect contractors who take on apprentices and help them get their training and hours. But are those young people working without direct supervision? I hope not, and I've seen more than a few bad renovations that were sold by the contractor, who then left the young, inexperienced labourers to do the job—badly, and sometimes dangerously.

It's a fact that when demand is high for contractors there's more bad work being done. That's because there are only so many good, experienced contractors available, and many homeowners who are anxious to get started on their home renovation just won't wait. They'd rather take a chance and play the slot machine of bad contractors. And when the economy heats up and more workers flood into an industry to find work, injuries rise. The new guys sometimes get inadequate safety training, and everyone's rushing and careless. It's a bad combination: inexperienced workers, potentially dangerous workplaces, and no safety equipment or training.

Your home, while it's under renovation, is considered a workplace. If an injury occurs due to unsafe practices, it's possible that you could also be charged and fined, and your job site shut down.

Your renovation project needs to be protected against delay and additional cost. You need to be protected against liability. But most importantly, the crew working on your house needs to be protected against injury. Make sure your contractor works safely.

Should you kick your contractor off the job?

I often hear from renovating homeowners who are fed up with their contractor and want to kick them off the site. Usually by then the situation is so bad and the anger and frustration so overwhelming that I can't believe there was ever a civilized word between them. So my first thought is, "How did you let it get this bad?"

Before you start yelling, check your contract. Read it again before you do anything. Look for what lawyers call "the limitations of liability" that are imposed on the contractor: the timetable, the types of materials used, the pricing for extras. Then look at the situation you're in as objectively as you can and ask, "Has the contractor actually violated any of the limitations?"

Ask yourself if it's a substantial violation. It's a big deal to kick your contractor off the job. You can't do that for a minor mistake like painting a wall the wrong colour. It better be for something a lot bigger, like not complying with building or safety bylaws, being significantly late on the schedule compared to the original plan, or billing more than agreed for an extra—without an acceptable explanation.

Don't be surprised if you find out that—no matter how angry you are—your contractor hasn't broken the agreement. And don't be surprised that even if it appears they have broken the agreement, your case against them isn't as black and white as you believe.

Here's an example of what often happens: You discover the contract requires the contractor or their representative to be working on-site at least three days a week and you haven't seen either of them for two weeks. Got him, you think! But then you read the rest of the contract, which allows your contractor an exception if they can claim there have been delays as a result of changes you made to the scope of work that have disrupted the schedule. You did make changes, didn't you? And the contractor did say they would disrupt the schedule, right? Well, whose fault is it then? And are you justified in kicking your contractor off the job?

Let's say you really have found something substantial. The contract will have something to say about how you're allowed to respond. Usually, contracts will require you to notify your contractor of your objection in writing and then give them time to make it right. You have to follow the instructions laid out in the contract before you can do anything drastic.

So start sending your notifications, and do two other things:

1. Have a job log where you can record the offences.

2. Bring in another contractor or quantity surveyor as a third party who can make your case from an expert's point of view. I have to say you should have started the log from the beginning of the job, especially if you're dealing with a bunch of little violations over time, but it's never too late to start.

With that, you're all set to give notice to the contractor. But don't expect it to be over. In fact it's just beginning, and what you now have on your hands is potentially years of court hearings and lawyer's fees, which gets me back to my first question: How did this happen? What did you do to let it get this bad? Being in this situation is like the guy nailing plywood over his windows in the middle of the hurricane. There's always, always plenty of warning. What were you so busy doing that you didn't see the clouds on the horizon?

Remember, we're not talking about fraudulent activity. This is two people starting on a project with good intentions in good faith and with a clear understanding of what's involved.

Or was it? Were your intentions good? Did you hire the contractor with the lowest price knowing they weren't going to get the necessary permits? Did you act in good faith? Were you already thinking you could beat the holdback out of the contractor if you complained enough when the project was done? Did you completely understand what was involved, or did you just stop listening and hope nothing bad would happen when the contractor said there could be complications once they started digging?

Don't find yourself trying to cover your windows in a hurricane. Look at the horizon and read the weather forecast.

The final walk-through

It's easy to be exhausted at the end of a renovation—especially a long one. You just want it to be over so you can move back in and move on with your lives.

But no matter what, you still need to go through and list everything that isn't completely satisfactory. This list becomes the centrepiece for getting the job finished like it should be. You will identify incomplete work or work that's been done improperly, oversights by your contractor, or defects in the materials.

Don't forget—your contractor is moving on too. They have other jobs to go on to and won't like being called back for each little fix-up you come across in the weeks ahead. They need to wrap up your job so they can move on to the next—they've got to make a living, after all. Do it efficiently—make a list.

Many people feel uncomfortable about going over deficiencies with their contractor—they may have established a sort of friendship with the contractor and feel awkward "forcing" them to fix things they aren't satisfied with—or worse, withholding payment until those things are fixed.

Don't. Your contractor won't be surprised to find you aren't willing to make the final payment on the contract until everything is satisfactory—that only makes sense to a professional.

At the close of a renovation, the contractor should call you (and your architect or representative and anyone else who has a stake in the success of the project) for a walk-through to identify anything that remains to be done, isn't up to standard, or has some defect that needs attention. If the contractor doesn't call you to set this up, by all means take the initiative and set up the meeting yourself.

Your contractor should have the latest set of plans with them and a long checklist of things to look at. This walk-through is your chance to bring up anything that concerns you. You're looking for flaws in the paint or drywall, odd-looking spots on the ceiling where the stucco is badly done—anything that doesn't look right. You'll look at the transition between the old and the new work. You'll test whether the doors open and close properly. You'll be trying any taps or toilets that have been installed.

When your renovation is complete, walk through it carefully and detail any outstanding work that may need to be done. Take your time and take photos if you need to.

The furnace should be turned up (or the air conditioning in the summer) so you can hear it running. Listen to how the ductwork responds to the load, and feel the air blowing from the registers. Look at the joints in the baseboard trim, the corners where the walls meet, and the cleanliness of any tile surfaces.

Check behind things. Run your hand over any built-in cabinetry. Is the finish to the standard you were told to expect? Trace the plumbing pipes as far as you can in the basement and satisfy yourself the installation is neat and clean.

If you're starting to think the walk-through might take a while, you're right. Depending on the size of the project, you should expect to spend between four hours and a full day doing it. The goal is to subject all the installations to normal use to see how they stand up. However, if you've been doing your job as a homeowner, you're already familiar with the guts of the job—that is, everything under the surface. At this point, your inspection should mainly be about cosmetics.

Ask lots and lots of questions. If you have an architect involved, lean on their expertise to help you understand what you're seeing. If you don't, you should consider having a third-party expert (a home inspector, or another contractor hired as a consultant) to be your advocate. As you go through the house, the contractor should be making notes, marking up the plans, and filling out their checklist where there are issues, but you should be making your own notes too. A tape recorder might be handy for you to help remember what you talked about.

If the list of deficiencies is long, give the contractor a couple of weeks to clean them up and try again. Whatever you do, don't rush. Make sure you're happy. It's your best chance to make sure the work done is done right.

Don't make that final payment to your contractor until you're 100% satisfied with the work, and until the contractor has provided you with a final invoice showing the amount has been paid in full. It goes like this: invoice first, then inspection, then satisfaction, and then final payment released (this is not the holdback). If this process continues too long, it might be wise to put the money in trust to show that it's actually there, and that you aren't just stalling for time because you're broke.

"Substantially complete"? Now hold back 10%

I've mentioned the importance of having a holdback clause in your contract from the outset. The holdback is the last 10% of the total value of the contract you "hold back" from the contractor after the job has been substantially completed. Most homeowners think the holdback exists to make sure the contractor comes back to finish the job. They're wrong.

The holdback exists to protect you from liens—by the contractor, the subtrades, or suppliers—against your property. Most provinces across Canada provide contract law which says you have 45 days to pay the last 10% of the contract price on your renovation once you agree the work is substantially done.

Your contractor—or the subtrades—have 45 days from substantial completion of your job to file a claim of lien against your property. You need to wait that 45 days for the time limit to expire before you fully pay out your contractor.

The holdback is not your insurance that things will be done right—the payment schedule is. I always tell people to build the payment schedule on their job around benchmarks. Once the contractor reaches a certain stage of completion, you release more money.

If you're unhappy with the way the job is progressing, stop paying the general contractor until things get back on track. It doesn't matter what kind of contract you have, whether it's a fixed price, or time and materials, or a project management contract. If the contractor isn't performing up to their standards, or more importantly, your standards, hold back any further money until you can rectify the situation.

The holdback clause, on the other hand, is designed to protect the subtrades who do the work and then don't get paid. It's to make sure they aren't ripped off by the contractor for the work they've done.

Sometimes a contractor will satisfy the terms of the contract, and the homeowners are happy with the finished job. But the contractor will "forget" to pay the subtrades, and they're left holding the bag. Their only recourse is to lien the house—your house—in an attempt to get paid by the homeowners what they're owed. And a subtrade or supplier who hasn't been paid has the right to put a lien on your property for 45 days after the job is substantially completed.

No, it's not fair. But your house is where they've invested their labour and materials. They have a stake in it.

If a lien is filed against your property, you can't sell that property until the lien has been paid or discharged. It's a legal claim against the value of your home. If you've paid the entire contract amount to the contractor, but a lien is filed, you're still required to pay the liens out of your pocket. Having money held back allows you to clear the lien with the money that you set aside for the original contract.

"Substantial completion"

Once you agree with the contractor that the job is substantially done, meaning 97% of the job is complete, you may be asked to sign a certificate of substantial completion. It's at this point that you have to choose to sign or not to sign, to agree or not to agree, based on how happy you are with the work. If you're not happy, you don't sign.

Many customers feel intimidated determining substantial completion, even if the contractor is being perfectly professional. It's normal to feel pressure to get everything over with as the job nears its end. But if you bring up your concerns as they come up during the renovation, there won't be any surprises for you or your contractor at the end.

Until the time limit for filing a lien has passed, make sure you hold back the final payment. The law says you have 45 days, so make sure you take them—no matter how much you like your contractor, no matter how happy you are with the renovation, no matter how much you believe the contractor will be back to finish the job.

Take that 45 days to make sure the job is done, that you're satisfied with the work, and that the subtrades have all been paid by the contractor.

Your end of the bargain: How to be a great client

I get many e-mails from frustrated people who tell me that they've had all kinds of contractors look at their job and then never even quote on the project. In the end, the person they decide to hire isn't their first choice, or even their second or third choice, but the one—the only one—who agreed to take the job. It's a frustrating start to what will likely be a lousy renovation.

So why does this happen? Wouldn't you think a contractor wants to work, that they want to take on your renovation job? This is going to sound harsh, but maybe it's not them. Maybe it's you. Maybe your job isn't a good one, and there are lots of possible reasons for that.

Homeowners need to understand that good contractors want to make sure the job is right for them, too. For good contractors—the ones with the right attitude and the ones that take pride in their work—this job is also about their next job. Good contractors know they're really only as good as their last project. Their reputation matters and referrals from satisfied clients are important.

Keep this in mind: The next time a contractor comes to look at your renovation, they're looking at what you want and need, and whether they can successfully deliver it given your budget, expectations, and timelines, and who else is working on the job. If they feel they might have to compromise their standards of quality—let's say your budget expectations are too low or you want the job rushed or you've hired some subtrades who aren't skilled—they'll walk away from your job.

This is a great time to be honest with your contractor. As much as you need to make a good decision, let your contractor have as much information as possible. Let them know your honest expectations and help them to help you—maybe what you're thinking about isn't realistic within your budget. A good contractor will let you know that, and if you aren't open to hearing so, they'll walk away. A bad contractor will promise to give you what you ask for, even if it's impossible.

Remember the contractor has to deal with suppliers, inspectors, engineers, and subtrades every day. That's the world your contractor lives in. They can't afford to damage those relationships for a project that they can see, going into it, is unrealistic.

I hear good contractors refer to their work as "my plumbing" or "my wiring" or "my roofing"—it shows they take pride in the work they do. They feel a sense of ownership and responsibility for the project. And they won't commit to a job that they know will be a problem, that they won't be able to feel proud of, and that might end up badly.

The homeowner and a good contractor are both looking for the same basic thing—a good job. The homeowner wants to look at their completed renovation and know they got value for their time and efforts, and take pride in the results. So does the contractor.

Be honest with prospective contractors about your expectations, and be realistic about how much it's going to cost, and you're more likely to find the good contractors lining up to work for you, instead of having to chase them down.

Questions to ask contractors

You want your prospective contractor to ask a lot of questions, but you need to ask a lot too, so that you avoid the nightmare of hiring the wrong contractor. Ask these questions and more:

1. **How long have you been working as a contractor?**
2. **Do you specialize in one area?**
3. **Who looks after getting permits?**
4. **How many jobs does your company have in progress right now?**
5. **Who will be on-site and in charge of my job each day?**
6. **Do you have a portfolio that shows insurance, certifications, a licence, and photos of the work you've done?**
7. **Who will be doing the electrical, plumbing, and insulation on the project?**
8. **Do you have a list of references?**

Questions to ask references

Don't skip this step. Call your contractor's references—all of them—and ask lots of questions. Better yet, go see the contractor's work. Some questions to start with:

1. **Did the contractor start and finish on time?**
2. **Did the contractor charge you money at the end of the job that you didn't expect?**
3. **Was the contractor courteous and clean?**
4. **Did the contractor keep you involved in the project by explaining what they were doing or telling you when something unexpected happened?**
5. **Did the contractor get permits?**
6. **Can I visit your home to see the work the contractor completed?**

CHAPTER 5

Greening Your Renovation

More and more homeowners want their renovation to be as green as it can be, and I think that's great. It's also the right thing to do. There are a lot of green options to choose from, but it's important to understand there are different shades of green—and decide for yourself if you want to be light or dark green.

Different products use the word "green" as part of their marketing strategy, and in truth a lot of it is crap. A lot of that stuff isn't "green" at all. When we use green products in our building we want to make sure we go "dark green"—which means understanding what's really "green."

What's really "green"?

Green building is about systems and integration. You need to think about the whole life of the project. If a building material you'd like to use isn't biological—biological means it completely biodegrades and decomposes without affecting the natural environment—then it should be a non-toxic and non-harmful synthetic that lasts a long time and has no negative effects on the environment.

That's a lot to ask of a product, and a lot to expect a homeowner to learn. How much is the average homeowner supposed to understand? Isn't it tough enough managing your renovation, finding a good contractor, and keeping your project on track? It comes down to how committed you are to the environment.

Who's going to pay for it?

Many green home construction features have a higher upfront cost than standard products, but you'll often save money in the long run because you'll be buying better quality and will have a more energy-efficient home in the end.

People who are into renovations for a quick buck won't be the ones to invest in some green technology that will take years to pay back. Just one more reason among many why I've never been a fan of the idea of flipping houses for profit. I think people should invest in their house and make it their home. In fact, I think one of the problems with new houses today is that people buy them without planning on staying there. If we did, the houses would be built differently; they'd be built to last. Odds are that every renovation puts some more material into a landfill somewhere, which is a good reason to make sure that your reno lasts.

What makes it green?

Saying something is "natural" doesn't necessarily make it good. Asbestos is natural. So is mould. It's a good idea to look for third-party certifications—EcoLogo, Green Seal, and Green Label are great—because you know the product has been tested and has passed.

There are lots of reasons a product can be called green. For instance:

- **It's made of recycled or salvaged material.**
- **It uses environmentally safe and health-safe materials.**
- **It lasts a very long time and won't need to be replaced soon.**
- **It's made with a rapidly renewable resource that can be harvested frequently (such as straw bales or bamboo).**
- **It has low or no emission of toxic chemicals into the air. (See more on low-VOC products on page 126.)**
- **No toxins result from its manufacture.**
- **It saves energy and water.**
- **It uses renewable energy.**
- **It can be recycled at the end of its useful life.**
- **The cost of transportation is low (made locally, lightweight, can be built on location).**

But there are other questions to ask yourself: How is the material grown, harvested, processed, shipped, and transported? Some products are green, but are they green across their entire lifecycle? For example, some woods claim to be green for flooring because wood is a renewable resource. But maybe that fact is offset by improper forestry techniques and the long distances that wood has to travel to find its market.

MIKE'S TIP

Green wood

One of the easiest ways to help green your renovation is by choosing the right lumber.

FSC-certified wood is not hard to find; it's in big box stores too. Forestry practices are monitored by the Forest Stewardship Council (FSC).

Engineered wood, one of my favourite products, is made from fast-growing "weed" trees (ash and poplar) and compressed under high pressure. The wood is strong and solid—great for structural beams.

One of the greenest woods is actually blue. BluWood is coated to protect against moisture and insects, so it's a good choice where these are issues.

Whatever you choose, good contractors plan carefully and pay attention to lumber dimensions so they only order as much wood as they need to minimize waste. And that's thinking green.

Natural products are not automatically green either. A house made of 100% wood—a log cabin, for instance—would be very green, since it's all organic. But wood isn't a great insulator and that house will lose a lot of heat in winter. It's not energy efficient, so how green is it?

Recycled?

Some products are recycled and recyclable. That's a great selling feature, but maybe it's not such a great product in the end—maybe it won't last long. Maybe it's only partly recycled.

Does it use post-consumer or post-industrial materials in its manufacture? It's greener if the recycled material is post-consumer waste, instead of post-industrial waste, since consumer waste is more likely to end up in a landfill.

The bottom line is that you have to read the fine print and check out the facts before accepting the "recycled" label as fact.

How green are you?

As I said, there are shades of green. Some people are committed to being energy-efficient and resource-efficient and building with locally available, sustainably harvested, renewable resources that are non-toxic. That's the greenest you can be.

Other homeowners may decide to build with conventional materials but finish with natural fibre carpets, energy efficient appliances, and low-VOC paints.

As you plan the detail of your attic or basement renovation, you need to determine how committed you are to being environmentally responsible during every phase of your project, including the initial tear-down.

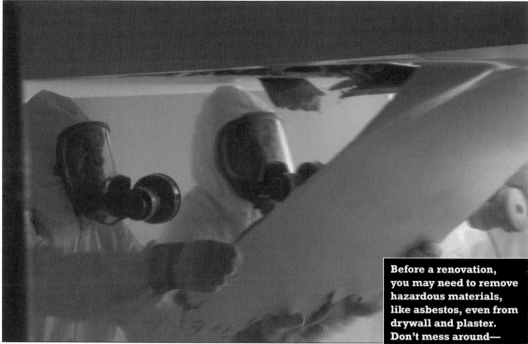

Green demolition: The three Rs at work

Any renovation project will create waste, and that can be a huge problem. Canada produces more solid waste per capita than many other countries, and waste from construction, renovation, and demolition accounts for about one-third of that waste. Talk about stress on the environment.

If you and your contractor agree to incorporate the three Rs (reduce, reuse, and recycle) into your reno project, you're making a significant contribution to the environment. You'll reduce the waste that goes to landfill sites. And by finding ways to reuse or recycle materials, you'll help to reduce the need to extract more raw materials for building.

What can you do?

First of all, plan for waste management. Find out where various materials can be reused or recycled, and make arrangements for pickup or drop-off in advance of your demolition. Some items will need to be stored on-site as you work, so make sure you have bins or other storage containers planned for these.

MIKE'S TIP

Making use of salvage

Check your local re-use centres, like the Habitat for Humanity ReStore, for things that you might be able to use in your reno. Sometimes these centres also get surplus overstock, factory overruns, and excess inventory or end-of-line products from manufacturers that you can buy for a fraction of the regular retail price.

There are a lot of advantages to reusing old building materials. For one thing, the purchase price will be lower than buying new off the shelf or custom. There's the environmental savings we all get from recycling. And sometimes older, weathered-and-worn materials can give a renovation project a special look that you can't get with new fixtures and materials.

You need to be aware of the real differences between surplus new, used, and antique before you start shopping, though. For instance, antique windows with single panes of glass won't have much thermal value, so they're probably not a sensible idea. You might use them as a decorative element, but not in place of energy-efficient windows. A better idea if you're looking to save on windows would be to search the re-use centre for surplus new models that might be perfect for your renovation needs.

In the case of salvaged wood, you may have better luck. A lot of wood used in old buildings was large, first-growth timber of a quality that is just not available now. It can be very stable, with few knots, and comes in larger dimensions than anything being sold today. The patina of age can add beauty to wood and add character to a project's look, whether it's flooring, cabinetry, wall panelling, or even furniture. You may not be able to use salvaged lumber for anything structural, but I bet you'd have a hard time matching the beauty of salvaged wood mouldings or a fireplace mantel, no matter how much time and money you spent.

It's important to understand that not everything can be reused. For example, lead paint can make an old piece of timber a health liability. If you find old lighting fixtures, you'll have to take them to a professional electrician to make sure they're safe to use and wired up to current code.

What can be reused?

Building materials in good condition can often be reused. Examples are acoustical ceiling tiles, doors, light fixtures, and cabinetry.

There are many companies that deal in used building materials. Look in the Yellow Pages under "Building Materials, Used" to find companies that will pick up your salvage, or contact one of the fifty-eight cross-Canada locations of the Habitat for Humanity ReStore. It's not hard to find someone who will take your used building materials off your hands. One person's trash is another's treasure.

What can be recycled?

Some items can't be reused, but they can be recycled. Scrap metal (including old wiring) is a prime candidate for recycling, and there are many metal recyclers across the country, in almost every major centre. Wood waste, drywall, asphalt shingles, concrete, and carpeting are all recyclable as well. Even the earth you pull from the ground for a foundation can be hauled away, as long as it's clean fill.

There are also a growing number of "mixed" recycling operations for construction, renovation, and demolition waste. These outlets will allow contractors to place different kinds of waste in a single waste collection bin, which reduces space and labour requirements on-site. There's a charge (usually per tonne) for handling waste in this way, however.

What's it going to cost?

There's a cost to getting rid of real waste—the stuff that's left over after you've recycled—at a landfill. The more you can divert through recycling or reusing, the

Much of the waste from a renovation can be recycled, including drywall and metal, so it's worth separating it from landfill.

MIKE'S TIP

Handling hazardous waste wisely

Hazardous materials are part of almost every demolition site. These materials require special handling. Contact your municipality to find out how and where these items can be safely disposed of:

- fluorescent light tubes and compact fluorescent tubes that contain mercury vapour
- paints that contain lead
- fluorescent light ballasts that contain PCBs
- lead sound barriers
- ceiling tiles with asbestos fibres
- air conditioning units with ozone-depleting substances
- drywall with asbestos
- insulation (asbestos) and pipe wrap

less you will spend on landfill fees. Yes, it will probably mean more time on the job site to take the room apart carefully rather than tearing it out, but some research shows that the added labour costs are offset by the reduction in fees combined with the money you'll make from selling used materials such as metal for reuse.

At the beginning of the job is a good time to ask a prospective contractor how they plan to handle the waste from your job site. It's another way to see if your contractor's principles and style match yours.

Green design

Green design includes many things. For example:

- **greater energy efficiency (programmable thermostats, increased insulation, a better-constructed building envelope, energy-efficient windows and doors)**
- **improved indoor air quality (hardwood or tile instead of carpet, no- or low-VOC materials, high-efficiency furnaces)**
- **water conservation (recycling rainwater for landscape irrigation/ car washing to reduce load on sewer system; low-flow showers and toilets)**

Strategically placed windows can provide passive solar heat in winter, and give you enough ventilation to reduce or even eliminate the need for air conditioning in the hot months of the year. Sometimes the windows you add during a renovation can help you get closer to this goal, too.

The first step to increase energy efficiency is to add or improve insulation, caulking, and weatherstripping wherever possible. Next on your list should be double-glazed/Low-E windows and high-efficiency appliances. The money you spend on better insulation and windows will start saving you money right away on heating and cooling bills.

Other energy upgrades include installing solar water preheaters, photovoltaic panels, or getting "green power" generated from renewable sources like the sun, wind, and geothermal energy (the earth itself).

All about volatile organic compounds

If you want a green renovation, you need to make sure the products you use are low-VOC (volatile organic compounds). VOCs are basically chemicals, such as formaldehyde, that are byproducts of many building supplies and products. They evaporate quickly into your indoor air—that's why they're "volatile"—and can affect your air quality. They can cause dizziness and headaches, eye irritation, and asthmatic reactions—and at high concentrations they can be toxic. Millions of people are chemically sensitive, and even low levels of VOCs can make them really sick.

VOCs are emitted from all kinds of products you'll use in a renovation—treated wood products, insulation, adhesives, carpets and other types of flooring, paint, cabinets, and furniture. VOCs are also an issue with products used on the exterior, with asphalt shingles being a great example. On one roof, the off-gassing of petrochemicals might not mean much, but when you multiply that by thousands or even hundreds of thousands of roofs, it's obviously a problem. Steel is a better choice for the environment, and it performs better too.

Newly constructed homes that have just been renovated have higher-than-normal levels of VOCs. Those levels decrease over time as the VOCs evaporate into the air and the air is dispersed. Some products—like spray foam insulation—will cure quickly, and within a few days the VOCs are virtually gone or are at non-detectable levels. Other products—like pressed-wood cabinets—will off-gas for much longer. And if the material is exposed to high temperatures or high moisture levels, the level of emission will be higher.

If you're considering wood floors, reclaimed wood is an obvious green choice.

Make better choices

You need to talk to your contractor and do your homework so you can make informed decisions about indoor air quality when you select materials to use in your home. You need to find out what the product is made of and whether it off-gasses. The truth is many building products—especially man-made ones—do. Glass, ceramic tile, metal, stone, and other hard and inert materials don't release any VOCs.

For cabinetry or shelving of any kind, choosing solid wood over composite wood products that contain formaldehyde is a good idea. If you can afford it, go for custom solid wood cabinetry with a low- or zero-VOC finish. Consider tile, hardwood, or linoleum instead of vinyl flooring, or natural carpet instead of a synthetic.

All engineered and manufactured wood products are made with at least some adhesives and resins, and most of those will off-gas. That includes plywood, oriented strand board, laminated beams, medium-density fibreboard, and particleboard. If these building materials are used in the framing and structure of the house, they'll be separated from the living space by drywall and plaster, which will help to some degree with off-gassing. The environmental upside of engineered lumber is that it's manufactured from "weed trees" (ash and poplar) that are fast-growing and easily replaceable, and the amount of glue used is actually quite small.

Paints and adhesives

Most paints contain VOCs because paints are formulated with solvents to improve their application or durability. But now you can find low- or no-VOC paints that have almost no odours as they cure. Be aware that the base paint might be low-VOC, but the tints that are added for colour might not be.

Water-based paints and adhesives have lower levels of VOCs than solvent-based products. And cleaning the brushes and equipment you use with oil-based paints involves using even more solvents, which go directly into the water supply, so water-based is the way to go.

How low is it?

You need to be careful when buying products and materials that say they're low VOC. The label might make that claim, but like calling a product "green" or "natural," it could mean anything. "Low VOC" from one company might just mean "lower than before," but it's still really high when compared with other similar products in the marketplace.

You need to buy products that have been tested and certified to emit low levels of VOCs. One standard to look for is the Green Seal. This says that a product has been rigorously evaluated and tested and meets certain standards that make it "environmentally preferable." In both Canada and the United States, the carpet manufacturing industry has created a Green Label to certify that certain carpets meet low-VOC requirements.

Following up: Checklist

Going green means figuring out where and when you're willing to choose the greenest options. Are you willing to sometimes pay extra, or work a little harder, to find the right products, in order to make environmentally friendly choices?

Your green priorities (check any that apply):

❏ **products made of recycled or salvaged material**

❏ **products that use environmentally safe and healthy materials**

❏ **products that last a very long time and won't need to be replaced soon**

❏ **products made with a rapidly renewable resource that can be harvested frequently**

❏ **low-VOC (or no-VOC) products**

❏ **products that don't create toxins during manufacturing**

❏ **products that save energy and water**

❏ **products that use renewable energy**

CHAPTER 6

Finishing Touches

When you're converting a basement or an attic, the really challenging parts of the job happen before the drywall goes up: structure, waterproofing, insulation, plumbing, and HVAC. By the time you've reached the finishing stage, you've made sure the structure is sound, you've got protection against moisture, and you've found ways to get water and conditioned air to these rooms. At this point, you should be able to treat these spaces like all the other rooms in your house.

But that doesn't mean you're done with challenges. Far from it. It's still wise to educate yourself about the finer points of finishing so that you can specify what you want, and guard against any mistakes or sloppiness.

Walls

When you look at a finished room, you probably don't think much about the walls. That's the way it should be: a wall that's been drywalled by a pro doesn't draw attention to itself. It's a flat, smooth surface without bulges, ridges, or imperfections. But that flawless finish doesn't happen by itself.

A well-finished wall begins with the framing. Studs should be selected carefully, with any warped or twisted studs weeded out. Your contractor should "crown" the studs—that is, make sure all studs are installed so the natural curve of the wood faces the same way. This is important to create an even surface for the drywall. When studs aren't crowned, you'll often see a waviness to the drywall, and probably some popped drywall screws over time.

Finishing drywall and installing trim takes real skill and is one area where you can really spot the work of a pro. It's not something you want your contractor to rush through or cut corners with.

You don't have to know everything about every type of drywall, but being a smart homeowner means knowing there's more to your walls than paint, and the right contractor for your home repairs and renovations is the one that knows their stuff when it comes to drywall.

Good contractors take the time to measure and order drywall carefully for a better finish. Drywall isn't just sold as 4' x 8' sheets. Varying lengths of drywall allow contractors to measure and order carefully to allow for the fewest possible tape lines when they lay the boards horizontally (not vertically) across the wall studs.

Paperbacked gypsum wallboard

Almost every home now is built with walls of ½" regular drywall made from gypsum covered with paper. It's the standard. It has some fire resistance, it's cheap, it meets code, and installed by an experienced tradesperson doing the taping and plastering, you'll get a nice finish.

But it's not the best choice everywhere in your house. Even ¾" drywall is a step up since it offers better sound and fire protection. There are all kinds of specialty boards that your contractor should discuss with you so you have the right drywall in the right place.

Fibreglass wallboard

Fibreglass drywall handles and looks like regular board, but has no paper so it can't be damaged by moisture. More important, without paper there's no food for mould spores. If there's anywhere in the home where mould might have a chance to grow—such as in the basement—I wouldn't consider using anything but paperless drywall.

If you have a mould problem, slapping up fibreglass board is not the solution, so don't accept anyone's suggestion that it might be. Mould indicates a problem with your building envelope—like a gap in the vapour barrier, failed insulation, or cracks in the foundation wall—that needs to be found and fixed.

Fibreglass drywall is more expensive and its surface of woven fibreglass is rougher than regular drywall too, so your contractor may need to apply a skim coat to get that nice finish you want.

As good as fibreglass board is, it's not the right choice for areas with constantly high moisture content like around shower enclosures in bathrooms. Cement board is a better bet.

Cement board

Cement board has a fibreglass facing like fibreglass board, but is cement, not compressed gypsum on the inside. The gold standard for tile backing is cement board. It's very stable, waterproof, and with a fibreglass facing you get the best of both worlds: no movement under the tile and no food for mould.

Green board

The economy, guaranteed-to-fail product is green board. It's supposed to be moisture-resistant, but I think it deserves the award for Most Useless Product in the Industry. Though there is some moisture resistance to the board, it's still covered in paper and will fail with anything but minimal exposure to moisture. Just don't use it.

Other specialty drywalls

There is drywall for bending around corners, drywall for high-impact areas of the home such as playrooms and hallways, and drywall that acts as a sound barrier. One

Installation matters.

Drywall is as much about the installation as the material. It's one area where you can really see the mark of a true professional. Don't hesitate to ask your contractor if he crowns his studs when he builds a wall. Is there solid backing at every seam where the drywall sheets meet? Tapered seams can extend 16 inches unsupported, but no more. Is there full backing on every inside corner? Does he do the ceiling first and then the walls? Is there a skim coat on fibreglass board for a cleaner finish? (The right answer to all these questions is "yes.") These questions will help you determine if your contractor will install the drywall correctly.

drywall manufacturer I know of has 14 different types of drywall and is constantly developing new ways of making its boards safer, more effective, and cheaper. Cost should not be your biggest concern, though, as some homeowners with Chinese drywall are unfortunately finding out. In 2009, some drywall from China was used in the United States and Canada that emits toxic hydrogen sulphide, sulphur dioxide, and other gases. Moisture in the air causes the drywall to off-gas, which smells and causes health problems like eye irritation, trouble breathing, and sore throat. It also can corrode exposed copper in your house, like pipes or wiring. Even a few sheets of this toxic drywall can contaminate your house and the only fix is to rip it all out. The lesson here is to not to be afraid to ask your contractor where the materials for your renovation are coming from and watch if the price is too cheap.

Ceilings

In most rooms including the attic, drywall is generally used for ceilings, but in a finished basement a suspended ceiling is a better choice.

Suspended or dropped ceilings are made of a metal grid that's attached to the floor joists and then ceiling tiles rest in the grid. A major advantage of a suspended ceiling is that it allows accessibility to junction boxes, plumbing, and electrical. You can easily remove a tile to check if there's a problem. And if a leak from upstairs drips down to the basement ceiling, you just need to replace a couple tiles rather than repair drywall.

If ceiling height is an issue and you can't spare the four to six inches of headroom that you'll lose with a suspended ceiling, ensure that you ask your contractor to install access panels in your drywalled ceiling so you can see junction boxes and can reach important access points like shutoff valves.

Your ceiling choices can help keep down the sound of footsteps and noise above your head. Using acoustic tiles instead of regular ceiling tile can help absorb sound. And doubling up your drywall on the ceiling or using a drywall specially designed for noise reduction can help too and won't cut into the height of your ceiling very much. Installing mineral wool insulation batts designed for soundproofing in the ceiling joists can help too. The insulation is denser than regular batt insulation, which makes it less effective as a thermal insulation, but helps cut noise and adds fire resistance between floors. If you plan to use pot lights in your ceiling, make sure that your light fixtures are rated IC (insulation contact) to help prevent fire.

Installation makes a difference too. Attaching the drywall on your ceiling to resilient channels, which are metal strips that run perpendicular to the floor joists, takes away a bit of ceiling height, but helps reduce the noise.

Using acoustic tile for basement ceilings allows for easy access to plumbing and electrical systems.

Trim

Trim may seem easy, and a lot of people—including DIYers and some so-called contractors—think they can buy a mitre box and some quarter round or baseboard and do it themselves.

But believe me, when it comes to having trim work (sometimes called millwork) installed, there's much more to it than meets the eye. If it's not perfect, your eye will notice every flaw. You can always tell professional-quality work.

Trim has a couple of purposes. The first is to protect the drywall from damage as a result of impact from vacuums and other household items.

What you see.
What I see.

People like pot lights. I say they don't belong in an attic at all. They give off a lot of heat (even if you use insulated ones), which affects your roof and ventilation.

You see a handy storage area in the attic that's separate from the living space. If it's not a conditioned space (heated or cooled) then it needs to be treated like a cold zone with a proper thermal break and an insulated door.

You see stairs off to the side, so there's more room in the centre of the attic. I'd want to make sure that there's enough headroom at the top of the stairs, which is a common challenge in attic renovations.

The second purpose is for looks. Trim covers up the rough edges of the construction and gives a finished look to windows, doors, and floor edges. Where the drywall meets the floor, there's a gap that needs to be covered with baseboard. The gap between your door framing and the drywall, the spray foam insulation around your windows—none of these are nice to look at, and trim is used to cover them up. Crown moulding on the ceiling may be more decorative, but it can tidy up a wall too.

If a coped joint isn't perfect—on an inside corner of some crown moulding, let's say—or if it moves and opens up over time, it will be very noticeable. What if your wall isn't quite true—does your finish carpenter know how to disguise it with trim? What if the walls aren't plumb, the floor isn't level, or your room is out of square? What if there's not enough blocking behind the wall to solidly nail the trim to? These are all issues that a skilled and experienced finish carpenter will know how to deal with.

Traditionally, trim was made of wood. It still is, but it can also be made of medium-density fibre board, plaster, or polyurethane. All of these have a place, and can be used to good effect by a skilled carpenter.

Custom mouldings may be needed if you're trying to match the style of one room to other rooms in your house. Is the house contemporary or does it need deep baseboards and built-up window and door casings to blend with the historic architecture? Using the narrowest, cheapest trims and mouldings will cheapen the whole effect of your reno, and make your newly finished room stick out like a sore thumb.

Finish carpentry is a skill that takes years of training to perfect. It also takes a good eye for proportion and detail. Unless you're a finish carpenter, do not kid yourself that you can do it, and make sure your contractor is either an experienced finish carpenter or has someone on their team who can do finish work. The money you've spent on a renovation will be wasted if the trim is badly done.

Painting basics

As you probably know, I always recommend hiring the pros—even when it comes to painting, which a lot of people think of as "the easy part" of the renovation.

If you're one of those people, I've got news: only a bad paint job is easy. A good paint job takes a lot of work, and most of that work happens long before you ever see a finish coat of colour on the walls. That's because the key to a great painted finish is thorough preparation of the walls and other surfaces to be painted.

For the best results, hire a professional painter to do the job, and follow their advice about what type of paint to use for specific applications. You'll still need to be involved when it comes to choosing colour and sheen, for instance, so here are some basics to help you along the way.

MIKE'S TIP

There are all kinds of paints available out there, with confusing names like acrylic and alkyd and so on. The two most basic—and most important—categories for the homeowner to know about are water-based paints and oil-based paints. They're formulated differently and have different pros and cons.

Water-based paints are known by a variety of names, depending on what goes into them: acrylic, vinyl, latex, or emulsion. They dry fast, so multiple coats can be applied in one day, and only water is needed to clean up brushes, rollers, or splatters. Like any paint, water-based paints have varying levels of durability, which match up with the "sheen" of the paint. You'll find that most water-based paints come in sheens that are called flat, matte, silk, satin, eggshell, semi-gloss, and high gloss (or some variation on these names). The more acrylic resins the paint contains, the shinier and more durable the finish.

Oil-based paints are tougher than water-based, although the durability of water-based paints is being improved all the time. That's fortunate, because oil-based paints (often called alkyd) are being phased out of the painting industry altogether. Not only do they contain flammable and toxic solvents, they require those same kinds of solvents to clean up brushes, rollers, trays, etc. The environmental impact that results from manufacturing these products, as well as the effects they have on air quality in the home, make it pretty clear why these products are on their way out. Even though you can still buy oil-based paints, for the sake of the environment and your own health, I recommend that you choose water-based paints instead.

Choosing the finish that's best for the job

Paint comes in a variety of sheen levels, from flat to high gloss, and each one is formulated for different applications. The lower the sheen level, the better the paint will

Floors at a glance

Material	Ceramic or porcelain tile	Cork	Hardwood	Engineered hardwood	Laminates (click flooring)	Bamboo	Carpet
Durability	Extremely durable	Fairly durable	Fairly durable	Fairly durable	Somewhat durable	Fairly durable	Depends on grade
Water-resistance	High	High	Low to moderate	Low to moderate	Low to moderate	Low to moderate	Low
Range of colours/patterns	Almost unlimited	Broad range of stain colours; patterns can be created	Broad range of stain colours; patterns can be created	Broad range of stain colours; patterns can be created	Broad	Broad range of stain colours; patterns can be created	Broad range of colours only
Cost	Moderate to high	Moderate to high	Moderate to high	Moderate to high	Low to moderate	Moderate to high	Low to moderate
Environmental concerns	Uses renewable resources; energy requirements to produce ceramic tile are high	Uses bark rather than whole trees; may be transported over long distances	Uses natural and renewable resources (FSC rating)	Uses some natural and renewable resources	Manufacturing process is not environmentally friendly	Uses a fast-growing, renewable resource; may be transported over long distances	Manufacturing process may not be environmentally friendly; carpet will off-gas in first months after installation
Good to know	Colour is throughout porcelain tiles so chips are less obvious	Naturally repels water and insects; resists mould; must be sealed	Can be resanded and refinished	May be resanded and refinished depending on thickness	Warranty may be void if used in a wet area	Installs much like hardwood	Needs a proper thermal break if used in a basement
Recommended by Mike	Yes	Yes	Yes	Yes	No	Yes	Yes

hide imperfections, and the better the walls will look. However, the lower the sheen, the less durable and washable the paint, so use flat paints with caution.

Flat or eggshell finishes are best for living areas and bedrooms, while a higher sheen is recommended for kitchens, bathrooms, children's rooms, and hallways. For baseboards and trim, semi-gloss is the best choice. Ceilings should be done in an ultra-flat, non-spatter ceiling paint.

So how do you get the look you want with the durability you need? First of all, it's essential that you buy top-of-the-line 100% acrylic paints. Most paint companies have a "kitchen-and-bath" paint that has a mildewcide and fungicides, and that's formulated with little or no starch or cellulose, which prevents water from penetrating. Higher-sheen paints are always the better bet against moisture.

Following up: Checklist for walls, trim, and paint

- ❏ If new stud walls and drywall are needed in your basement or attic, will your carpenter "crown" the studs, and use the right drywall for the job? Discuss this before the walls go up.
- ❏ For trim around windows, doors, and baseboards, think about the style that's needed to match other rooms in your house. For old houses, you might need custom-milled trim to get a good match. Make sure your contractor is an experienced finish carpenter, or has an experienced finish carpenter who can do trim work for you.
- ❏ What kind of paint is right for the different areas of your reno? Work with your contractor to figure this out. Consult a designer or decorator if you want help choosing colours.

Built to Last

I f you use the right products in your renovations and install them in the right way, then you've spent your money properly the first time and you may never have to renovate again. But you're not off the hook. The way we treat our homes is just as important as the way our homes are built. One home I worked on was owned by a wonderful old lady who loved to look after her home. After 60 years her bathroom was still in perfect shape.

Just like this lady did, you need to take care of your renovations and your home. If you have floors that need to be sealed regularly, keep that up. Look under sinks for water damage, change your furnace filter monthly, and regularly clean your ducts. Keep your house clean and check your drains regularly. And every year do a thorough inspection of the outside of your house, including looking at the caulking of your windows, checking the weatherstripping on your doors, cleaning your eaves troughs, and inspecting your roof.

Taking care of our homes will ensure that our homes outlast us, just like they used to. Years ago, skilled tradespeople built our country—they built the homes, the churches, the schools. Many of those buildings are still standing today. But the crap that we're building now isn't going to last a decade without costing a lot of money. That's because we don't care about our buildings anymore. It's no longer about craftsmanship. It's all about making money. In the past we built properly, but we're doing it wrong today and it needs to change. We need new minimum building codes for ourselves, for those who come after us, and for our environment.

New building codes might get rid of building without caring and building without knowing why we do things. It's not good enough to just know how to do things. We have to ask why. Understanding comes from knowing why, and we need to understand how buildings work. That way we can make them better, we can make them last, and we can make them last sustainably.

With the Holmes Foundation, I'm working to help train the next generation of skilled tradespeople so they understand how buildings work and how to build it right. Building it right means building it better by using better materials, more efficient techniques, and greener products. Professionals keep their minds open to improvements because not only do those improvements make their world easier, they make our world better, too.

If we think more about building for our planet and building for longevity, then we're building smart. We should be building homes with better lumber that's going to last longer, with better drywall that's not going to mould, and we should continue to build from the outside in and not the inside out. That means focussing on the structure, the roof, and the exterior of the building first and then the interior—the lipstick and mascara.

When we build from the outside in, we can properly think about building better than minimum code so that we build fireproof houses, mould-free houses, and watertight and truly green homes. Should we be focussing on this? Should we demand this? Well, why not? Do we really want something that's minimum code? The answer's no. Minimum code means it won't fall down. It doesn't mean it will outlast us or be good for the environment. Let's do better than minimum.

By doing better than minimum you can have the renovation of your dreams, one that you can enjoy for years to come. And by paying attention to what's underneath our renovations—like structure, plumbing, and electrical—updating your home down the road will be much easier. Do it right, take care, and your house should outlast you.

Attic or basement renovation: Step-by-step checklist

Step one: Preparation (one to three months)

- ❏ Start an ideas file. Buy a few folders to keep magazine clippings, pamphlets, product flyers, copies of your contract, any change orders that come up, etc.
- ❏ Take "before" photographs, and continue to photograph the job at every stage. Photos are helpful if you ever have a dispute with your contractor, or if you need proof of the work for your insurance company.
- ❏ Do preliminary plan drawings and basic product and material specifications, or hire a designer to help you create a design.
- ❏ Assess the existing space. Consult a general contractor or a home inspector to thoroughly inspect your house and give ballpark estimates on the plans you have in mind.

Step two: Hiring your general contractor (one to six months)

- ❏ Investigate at least six candidates using the same interview questions for each. Ask for referrals and follow up with phone calls and/or visits to previous projects. Submit copies of your plan drawings and basic material and product specifications to each contractor for written bids.
- ❏ Compare bids, qualifications (including licensing and insurance), and the results of referral checks for each contractor.
- ❏ Together with the contractor, finalize construction and design plans, including drawings and material specifications. Create a detailed contract that specifies the scope and cost of the project, complete material and product specifications, work and payment schedule, and contingency process ("extras").
- ❏ Make your first payment to the contractor never more than 10% of the total cost of the job.
- ❏ Determine who will seek building permits (you or the contractor). Ensure that all necessary building permits are obtained. Keep permits and inspection reports in a file folder at the job site for referral at any time. Post your permit notice in the window.
- ❏ Order any custom or special-order products, such as windows or cabinets.

Step three: Demolition and construction (one to two months)

- ❏ Prepare the space by removing furniture and personal belongings.
- ❏ Have your contractor seal off the construction zone with plastic sheeting.
- ❏ Begin demolition. Reuse or recycle where possible.
- ❏ Do any necessary structural repairs or reinforcements.
- ❏ Do any necessary waterproofing work on foundation exterior (for basement) and on roof system (for attic).
- ❏ Frame walls and doors.
- ❏ Install windows.
- ❏ Rough in the electrical circuits, plumbing, and duct work, followed by inspections.
- ❏ Insulate with closed-cell polyurethane foam insulation (or batt insulation and separate vapour barrier), followed by inspection.
- ❏ Install the subfloor (and in-floor heat, if using).
- ❏ Install finish flooring.
- ❏ Install drywall: tape, mud, and sand.
- ❏ Paint: primer and two finish coats.
- ❏ Install any built-in cabinetry and trim.
- ❏ Install any plumbing fixtures, followed by final plumbing inspection.
- ❏ Install electrical outlets and lighting fixtures, followed by final electrical inspection.
- ❏ Install other finishing touches.

Step four: Completion (six weeks)

- ❏ Do final walkthrough with contractor. Make a list of touch-ups needed, and monitor progress until all items are completed.
- ❏ Make payment due on "substantial completion." Hold back 10% until 45 days have passed and you have received proof that all subtrades and suppliers have been paid.

GLOSSARY

ABS (Acrylonitrile Butadiene Styrenesome). Hard black plastic plumbing pipes, used primarily for drainage. The rule of thumb for drainage pipes is ABS pipes in your house and PVC for in-ground pipes. Some municipalities forbid the use of ABS pipe for any application.

AFCI (arc fault circuit interrupter). An electrical device in your circuit panel that cuts power to prevent electrical fires when the AFCI detects minute differences in electrical current caused by punctured wires, shorts, and arcing. *See also* GFCI.

Amperes (or amps). An electrical unit of measurement that measures the rate of electrical charge flowing through the system. Electrical service panels and circuit breakers are usually measured in amps.

Arc. A short circuit where the electricity literally jumps or arcs to the nearest metal.

Batt. Fibreglass, mineral wool, and cotton insulation are usually sold in rectangular batts, a fluffy material (much like cotton candy). In walls, insulation batts are placed between studs.

Bay. The space between the rafters in an attic.

Beam. A wooden or steel member that runs horizontally in the opposite direction to the joists, helping to support the structure above.

Building code. The building code sets out the minimum standards for framing and foundations that will ensure that a house is going to be safe and secure. The code is fairly uniform across North America, though there are special provisions in some regions to protect against local dangers, such as earthquakes or hurricanes. Separate codes deal with a house's plumbing and electrical systems.

Building inspector. A municipal employee who inspects a home as it's being built or renovated to ensure that the work meets the minimum local building code.

Caulk/caulking. Flexible sealant that is used to stop air or water penetration. Caulk comes in many strengths and varieties. The most common caulks are made from latex and silicone.

Cement board. A harder, heavier and more waterproof alternative to drywall, concrete board is made from concrete sandwiched between two layers of fiberglass mesh. Concrete board is advisable for areas with heavy moisture since it will not mould like regular drywall.

Centres. Refers to the distance between the middle of two studs (or joists). For example, in modern houses, the distance from the centre of one stud to the centre of the next stud is usually 16", often spoken of as "16 inches on centre," or written as "16" o.c." This distance ensures adequate structural support, and the standard measurement allows for drywall or other coverings to be easily attached to the studs.

Cinder block. Often used in foundations, cinder blocks are made of concrete and coal cinders.

Circuit. Electricity flows in a circuit, from the service panel to various outlets and fixtures and then back to the panel. Each circuit is rated for amps, which are controlled by a circuit breaker, commonly 15 or 20 amps. A circuit controlled by a 20-amp breaker is capable of safely carrying 1,800 watts (20 amps x 120 volts x 80% (for safety). Ten outlets is usually the maximum for a circuit (fewer if those outlets are serving appliances that draw a lot of electricity, such as window air conditioners).

Circuit breaker. A protective device in an electrical panel that interrupts the flow of electricity in an electrical circuit when there is an excess load or a short. Older service panels used fuses, but they were replaced by circuit breakers, which are easier to reset.

Cold zone. An area within a house that isn't heated, such as an attic or crawl space. It's critical that cold zones have proper ventilation to avoid moisture buildup and rot.

Concrete. A construction material made from a mixture of cement, sand, stone, and water. There are many different types of concrete available, and it's critical to use the right one for the job and to not allow concrete to harden too quickly.

Crawl space. A shallow, unfinished space beneath the first floor of a building. Crawl spaces are sometimes built instead of full-height basements.

Crown. The natural bow in a piece of wood, a visible curve. It's critical when framing a house that all the crowns face the same direction. In a vertical wall, the crowns should face out; on the floor, the crowns should face up.

Ditra. A brand-name product from Schluter, Ditra is a waffled orange plastic material that is used under tile to help prevent tiles from cracking.

Drywall. The most common interior wall material, drywall is made from gypsum (a chalk-like mineral) sandwiched between two layers of heavy paper. Drywall comes in many different types and thicknesses, including denser drywalls for ceilings, fire-rated drywalls, and water-resistant and mould-proof drywalls for high-moisture areas.

Drywall compound. Often called "mud," drywall compound is a paste that is used to fill and cover the seams in drywall sheets.

Ducts. The round or rectangular sheet metal pipes in which air flows from a forced air furnace. The main duct from the furnace is called the plenum, and individual ducts run off the plenum to rooms throughout the house.

Efflorescence. A white, salty crystal-like deposit commonly seen on foundation walls. The presence of efflorescence is a sign of water invasion in basements.

Engineered wood. Hardwood flooring that is made of three to five layers of wood, stacked and bonded together under heat and pressure.

Fascia. A long, flat board fastened to the ends of the eaves on roofing rafters. This is on the exterior of the house.

Feed lines. Plumbing pipes in which water is supplied to the house or to an individual fixture (such as a sink or bathtub). Modern feed lines are usually copper or flexible plastic tubing.

Flashing. The thin sheet metal around the chimney, dormers, skylights, and so forth. In the case of the chimney, for example, the flashing rests flush against the chimney and then goes under the shingles.

Footings. Foundation walls rest on concrete footings, which in turn rest on undisturbed earth. Footings should be twice the width of the wall itself.

Forced air. A common form of heating, featuring a powerful fan that forces warm air throughout the house via ducts in the walls. Forced air furnaces can be powered by natural gas, electricity, propane, or oil.

Foundation. The foundation bears the weight of the house and holds up against the pressure of the earth around it. Foundations can be made of a variety of materials including fieldstone, brick, concrete block, poured concrete, and insulated concrete forms. Foundations are usually dug at least four feet into the ground, below the frost line.

Geothermal system. A heating system that captures heat from deep in the ground. Geothermal systems may be used to supplement more traditional home heating methods.

GFCI (ground fault circuit interrupter). This protects people from severe electric shocks and electrocution. A GFCI monitors the amount of current flowing from hot to neutral circuits; if there is a difference—even as small as 4 or 5 milliamps, amounts too small to activate a fuse or circuit breaker—it cuts the electricity in a fraction of a second. *See also* AFCI.

Header. In a wooden stud wall, the 2 x 4 above the window or door is called a header.

Home inspector. A person who, independently or in association with a small or nationwide home inspection company, inspects homes to assist potential buyers in making real estate decisions. Services usually include the inspection and a written report, and are charged on either a flat-rate or hourly basis.

House wrap. A house wrap sheds moisture from the outside even while it allows air to flow through its microscopic holes. The air movement allows moisture to move back through to the outside. The most popular house wraps are Tyvek and Typar.

HRV (heat recovery ventilation) unit. An HRV brings fresh air into the furnace and exhausts stale air. A heat exchanger in the HRV recovers heat from the outgoing air and preheats incoming air to help reduce energy costs.

HVAC. An acronym for the heating, ventilation, and air conditioning systems in a house.

Jack stud. A second vertical stud used to reinforce the structure of a stud frame wall where a door will be installed.

Joists. Horizontal, parallel beams, usually placed on their edge to support the floors and walls in a house.

Junction box. A metal box where separate lines are run off the circuit to receptacles and lights.

Kerdi. A brand-name product from Schluter, Kerdi is a membrane that can be used on floors and walls to create a waterproof barrier before installing stone, ceramic, or porcelain tiles.

Knob and tube. The oldest form of electrical wiring, which was installed until about 1945. The system featured two separate wires, one black and one white, for each circuit, unlike today's electrical wires, which combine black, white, and ground wires.

Knob and tube refers to the ceramic knobs the wire was strung from and the tubes used to protect the wire where it passed through joists and studs.

Laminate floor. A flooring system comprised of interlocking panels. Each panel is made up of an inner core of pressed and glued wood material, with a photographic image of wood (or some other pattern) laminated on the surface.

Lath. Before drywall became the common choice for interior walls, small slats of wood (lath) were nailed horizontally to the wall studs with a narrow gap between each piece of lath. Thick layers of plaster were then applied to the lath to make a smooth covering.

Lien. A legal claim made by one person on another person's property as security on a debt. A contractor (or subcontractor) may place a lien on a house when they have not been paid so that if the house is sold they are repaid from the proceeds.

Load-bearing wall. A wall that is integral to the construction of the house. It cannot be safely removed without building new supports that will bear an equal load; various solutions are possible.

Mastic. A cement adhesive used to fix tiles to floors, specifically vinyl and linoleum.

MDF (medium-density fibreboard). Because it doesn't have the structural strength of solid wood or plywood, MDF is not recommended in most renovations, but MDF crown moulding and trim are popular, lower-cost options.

Mould. A fungus that grows on organic materials such as wood or paper, especially when moisture is present.

Mud. *See* drywall compound.

Off-gassing. Off-gassing happens when chemicals are released into the air by a non-metallic substance, such as paint, varnish, or glue. Known as volatile organic compounds (VOCs), the chemicals in off-gases cause a wide range of impacts ranging from relatively mild—stinging eyes, irritated nasal passages, and nausea—to potentially life-threatening.

OSB (oriented strand board). A modern version of plywood that uses layers of wood flakes, fibres, or strands bonded together under intense heat and pressure. The direction of the fibres is alternated between layers for greater strength.

Plaster. Common in homes built before the 1940s, plaster is made from gypsum mixed with water and fibrous material. Horsehair was sometimes added to strengthen the plaster before it was applied over wooden lath in plaster-and-lath walls.

Plenum. *See* ducts.

PVC (polyvinyl chloride). Plastic used in plumbing pipes (usually white or grey). When it is used as a drainage pipe, PVC connects to the city sewer system or a septic system. When it comes to drain pipes, the standard rule is ABS for the vent stack and PVC for the in-ground drainage.

R-2000. Refers to homes built to a set of energy-efficient standards created by the Canadian government (Natural Resources Canada) and the Canadian Home Builders' Association. Only homes built by specially trained contractors, and conforming to the R-2000 Standard, can be certified as R-2000. Since these homes began to be constructed in the 1970s and 1980s, some problems have arisen, especially with airtightness that led to moisture and mould growth.

R-value. The R-value of any material—usually insulation—measures how well that material resists the loss of heat if the temperature on one side of it is higher than on the other side. Basically, the higher the R-value, the better the material insulates.

Rigid foam. Not to be confused with white Styrofoam, rigid foam is made from either extruded polystyrene (often seen as pink and blue boards) or expanded polyisocyanurate. Rigid foam is commonly used for insulating foundations and as a thermal and vapour break in basements.

Rough-in. In plumbing and electrical work, "rough-in" is the stage when an inspection by a building or electrical inspector should occur. The pipes or wires have been installed, but the walls and floors have not been closed in and the fixtures have not been connected.

Service panel. All electricity entering a house first goes into a service panel, a wall-mounted box, usually in the basement, which features breakers for individual circuits.

Soffits. The underside of roof eaves, visible from the ground. Modern soffits are perforated to allow for air movement.

Spalling. The flaking of concrete. A sign of poor quality material or application.

Stucco. A mixture of Portland cement, sand, lime, and water that can be used as a covering for exterior walls.

Stud. One of a series of wood or metal vertical structures in walls and partitions. Wood studs are usually 2 x 4s, though 2 x 6s are also used, especially for exterior walls, to allow for adequate insulation.

Subfloor. Attached to the supporting joists underneath it, the subfloor is as it sounds: what is below your floor covering. In older houses, the subfloor was often broad planks; in newer houses, it is usually OSB or plywood.

Sump pump. A sump pump commonly refers to both the sump box and sump pump. By code, new houses have a sump box (also known as a well or a pit) underneath the basement floor that collects water from your foundation walls and under your basement floor. When the box gets full, the sump pump takes the water up and out of the house by means of a pipe that goes through the foundation wall, and away from your foundation.

Thermal barrier. A material (such as plastic) used between warm areas (such as the interior of a house) and cold areas (such as the exterior, in northern climates) to lessen moisture buildup and heat loss.

Thermal break. A material (such as foam) that completely separates warm areas (such as the interior of a house) from cold areas (such as the exterior, in northern climates). Because cold and hot do not meet at all, there is no moisture buildup or heat loss. The best analogy is the structure of a beverage cooler: the built-in foam insulation acts as a thermal break to keep cold drinks completely separated from warm air outside.

Thinset. A mixture of cement, very finely graded sand, and additives that allow the cement to properly hydrate. "Modified" thinset has additional polymers added to improve adhesion—basically, thinset with more glue.

Truss. A prefabricated triangular roof support. Trusses come in a wide variety of sizes and shapes.

Typar/Tyvek. *See* house wrap.

Underpinning. When lowering a basement floor, underpinning creates a new, deeper footing (the widest part of the foundation, which the walls sit on) underneath the existing one.

Vapour barrier. Usually a 6-mil polyethylene plastic sheet, vapour barrier is stapled to the studs on the warm side of an exterior wall (usually this means the interior side of the insulation) to prevent water vapour from getting into the studding.

Vent stack. Also called "the stack" or the "waste and vent stack," the vent stack is a vertical pipe that carries water and waste down to the drainage pipe in the basement. Open at the top, and typically sticking out through the roof of your house, the stack also lets sewer gases escape and provides air for drains and toilets to empty properly.

VOC (volatile organic compounds). The chemicals in off-gases, which cause a variety of impacts ranging from relatively mild—stinging eyes, irritated nasal passages, and nausea—to potentially life-threatening.

Volts. An electrical unit of measurement that measures the electrical pressure exerted by a power source. In Canada, most electrical service is 120 volts or 240 volts.

Water table. The level below which the ground is saturated with water. The level of the water table varies from place to place and at different times of the year.

Watts. An electrical unit of measurement that measures the amount of electrical energy flowing to a particular fixture in an electrical system. All the lights and devices that you run off your circuits are rated for wattage—the amount of electricity they consume. You see this on light bulbs most obviously, but most home appliances—from toasters to TV sets to computers—also give their wattage.

Weeping tile. Not really tile anymore (the original drainage tile was made of clay), weeping tile is corrugated plastic piping with slits in the top. It is laid around the outside of the foundation to capture excess water and drain it away from the home. The weeping tile connects to the city storm drains. In the suburbs or rural areas, it may be collected into a sump well and then pumped out to ditches.

Acknowledgements

Last year, I had the privilege of being a part of the World Skills Competition in Calgary, where the best professionals from around the world competed. Their passion, precision, and craftsmanship was inspiring and a sign of a whole new generation of trades workers who take pride in their work and care about what they do. I see the same passion in our work with The Holmes Foundation and in the recipients of our bursaries and scholarships. I'm grateful to everyone who supports our foundation and its mission to ensure that all residential renovation and construction in Canada is done right—the first time.

My passion for the trades was inspired by my dad and his commitment to always make it right. Every day I get to work with people who share that belief. I always say that you're only as good as the people who surround you, and I get to work with the best, including my kids, Amanda, Sherry, and Mike—every father should be so lucky. To everyone at The Holmes Group, my greatest appreciation.

This book would not be possible without the commitment and insight of Liza Drozdov, Seth Atkins, Michael Quast and Pete Kettlewell. Special thanks to HarperCollins Canada, especially Brad Wilson, Nicole Langlois, Noelle Zitzer, Alan Jones, and Neil Erickson for their expertise, dedication, and passion.

Finally, to all the contractors who care about making it right, thanks and keep doing what you do.

Index